A Phaidon Theatre Manual

KT-134-650

A Phaidon Theatre Manual
LIGHTING
AND SOUND
NEIL FRASER

Series Editor: David Mayer

Acknowledgements
The author and the publisher gratefully acknowledge
the help and assistance of the students and staff at the
Royal Academy of Dramatic Art, London, for their par-
ticipation in the photographs taken by Michael Prior.
The author extends particular thanks to Mr Colin Brown,
and for past help thanks should also go to Wayne,
Clem, Jon, Francis, Andy, Ali and Paul. Thanks also to
the Contact Theatre Company, Manchester, especially
Barbara.

Photographs: Catherine Ashmore p. 63; Mick Hurdus
pp. 27, 120-125; Oxford Stage Company p. 55; Michael
Prior pp. 29, 31, 33, 35, 44-45, 51, 101, 111; Robert
Seatter p. 117; Solid State Logic p. 95; Theatre and TV
Lighting, Belgium p. 69.

Illustrations: Jones, Sewell and Associates pp. 13, 17,
19, 20-21, 28, 38, 39-41, 47-49, 57, 60-61, 65-67, 69-
75, 79, 85-89, 91-92, 105, 113-114; Miller, Craig and
Cocking p. 15.

Phaidon Press Limited
Regent's Wharf
All Saints Street
London N1 9PA

Phaidon Press Inc.
180 Varick Street
New York, NY 10014

www.phaidon.com

First published 1988
Revised edition 1993
Reprinted 1995, 1998, 1999, 2002, 2004

© 1988, 1993 Phaidon Press Limited

ISBN 0 7148 2514 X

A CIP catalogue record for this book is available from
the British Library.

Printed in Singapore

Contents

INTRODUCTION

Work in the theatre is always undertaken with a future performance in mind, but two artistic facts of life affect this work. One is that no one, no matter how naturally talented and accomplished, can invariably count on inspiration to solve a problem. The other fact is that time is the most precious of all theatrical commodities. The date of a first performance is an unalterable deadline, and that deadline, in turn, determines a whole sequence of earlier deadlines which must be met within the resources, not always ideal, that are available to the theatrical team.

These facts have been our starting-point in devising this series. Inspiration may be rare, but creativity, we suggest, can be supplemented by technique. Effective organization coupled with careful forward-planning can result in impressive productions. Experience has shown that good preparation will actually free the creative imagination and give it room to flourish.

This series has been designed to meet the needs of those working in the non-professional theatre, that is students and undergraduates, school teachers, and members of amateur dramatic and operatic societies. This is not an indication of the standards of the performances to be achieved; some amateur productions are quite outstanding. In fact some of the differences between the amateur and the professional are in the amateurs' favour: amateur groups can often call upon enormous resources for behind-the-scenes labour and the large casts that are so often out of reach of most professional companies. But non-professionals are more likely to be limited by the amount of time, money, space and materials available. We recognize that you will be working with some or all of these advantages and restrictions, and we offer ways of looking at problems which will stimulate the imagination and produce solutions. The answers will then be yours, not ours.

Putting on a play is essentially teamwork, teamwork which depends upon the creativity of administrators and craftsmen, performers, directing staff and stage crews. The team can best thrive when responsibilities are shared and lines of communiciation are always open, direct and cordial. In recognition of these needs we have linked the books by planning charts and repeating themes looked at from different angles in order to emphasize that the best results are always achieved when skills are pooled.

Dozens of performances and hours of discussion lie behind these texts, and while we cannot claim to have covered every eventuality, we are confident that the approach outlined in the following pages will lead to productions that are successful, imaginative, and, above all, enjoyable for you, your colleagues, and your audiences.

David Mayer

Safety

Attention to safety is vitally important when you are putting on any production. When there is a procedure in this book where special care must be taken a safety flash ▲ *has been inserted in the margin.*

Dear Reader, Books by Phaidon are recognised world-wide for their beauty, scholarship and elegance. We invite you to return this card with your name and e-mail address so that we can keep you informed of our new publications, special offers and events. Alternatively, visit us at **www.phaidon.com** to see our entire list of books, videos and stationery. Register on-line to be included on our regular e-newsletters.

Subjects in which I have a special interest

☐ Art   ☐ Contemporary Art   ☐ Architecture   ☐ Design   ☐ Photography

☐ Music   ☐ Art Videos   ☐ Fashion   ☐ Decorative Arts   ☐ Please send me a complimentary catalogue

	Mr/Miss/Ms	Initial		Surname
Name				
No./Street				
City				
Post code/Zip code			Country	
E-mail				

This is not an order form. To order please contact Customer Services at the appropriate address overleaf.

Please delete address not required before mailing

Affix
stamp
here

PHAIDON PRESS LIMITED

Regent's Wharf

All Saints Street

London N1 9PA

PHAIDON PRESS INC

7195 Grayson Road

Harrisburg

PA 17111

Return address for USA and Canada only

*Return address for UK and countries
outside the USA and Canada only*

CHAPTER 1

UNDERSTANDING THEATRE

INTRODUCTION

This book is an introduction to the art of theatre lighting and sound. It can be used by the novice who aims to become expert, or by the experienced technician to improve working methods, pick up new ideas and skills, and confirm old ones. It can be read as a whole or dipped into for specific references. The glossary and index at the end of the book make this particularly easy. The book is designed to give readers instant access to information and ideas.

Theatre is about teamwork rather than isolated ideas and talents. Knowledge of equipment and techniques is only half the technician's skill. The other half is the ability to work with others and understand their thinking. Without that, all the technical knowledge in the world is of little or no use. Teamwork is the essence of the *drama* itself and it is also why working in theatre is so rewarding.

A needless mystique surrounds many aspects of theatre, and some theatre people keep this alive by being deliberately vague about *what* they do and *how they do it*. Of course, there *is* something magical about the play, the finished product, but its creation is just like that of any other human endeavour; a combination of skill, knowledge and effort. There is nothing unusually clever or mysterious about it. This book gives you the knowledge and shows you how to acquire the skills. The hard work is up to you.

WORKING METHODS

References throughout this book are to common theatre working practice. A sample production schedule on the next few pages shows how the elements described here fit in with the work of all other departments in the business of mounting a theatrical production.

In the modern theatre the technical elements now play as important a role as any other single element of the production, except, of course, that of the actor. Traditionally, the set designer held the senior position among the technical team. The sophistication of modern equipment means this needs rethinking. Before the modern age the scenic designer could create a magical world on stage with paint and canvas, while the lighting and sound effects could only support this work. Today the scenery, lighting and sound can all create equally astounding special effects and atmospheres.

Although the first sections of this book deal with purely technical information, bear in mind that this is only a means to an end. The essence of the book is about creating credible unimagined worlds out of the darkness of the empty theatre space using light and sound.

Working in this way the theatre technician can help transform the thoughts of the director or playwright into reality. Like the actor, the technician has the power to breathe life into ideas!

A single 1 kw floor lantern provided the shadows for this production of Brecht's Arturo Ui. As the play progressed Ui was caught in this lantern at points further and further down stage – his shadow grew and grew until it filled the entire back wall!

Pre-production Period

Function	Pre-rehearsal Period
Administrator	Check play available for performance. Check score available for performance. Check venue available. Negotiate royalty payments. Pre-production discussions with Director and Designers. Check licensing and permission, especially firearms. Check credit card registration. Gather programme material. Plan publicity. Announce auditions. Determine budget.
Director	Pre-production discussions. Conduct auditions – with choreographer and Musical Director. Announce casting. Announce and initiate rehearsal schedules.
Production Manager/ Technical Director	Pre-production budget meeting with Administration. Design meeting with Director, Designer and Stage Manager. Appoint Stage Manager and technical staff.
Stage Management	Attend design meeting and run auditions. Find a rehearsal space. Prepare prompt copy and provisional lists. Research with designer. Gather rehearsal props, furniture and set.
Scenic Design and Construction	Pre-production discussions. Model making: technical and working. Prepare drawings. Prepare prop drawings. Get Director's approval. Prepare castings and planning.
Lighting	Pre-production discussions. Read and re-read text. Research & Planning costume and scene.
Sound	Pre-production discussions. Read and re-read text. Prepare a selection of provisional tapes. Get Director's approval.
Music	Check availability of scores. Agree rehearsal schedule with Director. Organize a rehearsal pianist. Audition singers. Gather orchestra.
Choreography Fights	Check rehearsal space. Agree rehearsal schedule with Director. Organize rehearsal pianist. Audition dancers.
Costume Design and Construction	Pre-production discussions. Costume research and drawing. Working drawings for wigs/hats/shoes. Fabric sampling. Costing and planning.

Function	Week 6	Week 5	Week 4	Week 3
Administration	Gather programme material. Display publicity material. Open booking if necessary.	Start press stories. Monitor publicity. Monitor bookings. Contact with rehearsals.	Recruit FOH staff if required. Invite critics.	Direct sell.
Director	Attend production meeting. ■ Discussions ■ Script cuts ■ Note running time.	Blocking rehearsal.	Business rehearsals. Rehearsal props introduced. Attend meetings. Listen to sound tape. Lighting meeting	Singers and dancers integrated. Reblocking. ■ Pianist present. Orchestral rehearsal
Production Manager	Costing meetings with set, prop and costume makers. Production meeting. Problem solving and budget decisions.	Coordinating technical departments and budget control. →		Progress meeting. Arrange for equipment Liaison with venue.
Stage Management	Mark out and prepare rehearsal space. Note script changes. Attend production and props meetings.	Run rehearsal Prop, furniture and dressings search and making. Liaison with all departments.	←	Attend progress meeting Arrange sound and light meetings for director
Scenic design and construction	Meetings and planning with technical director. ■ Attend read through Call for actors, staff and workshop. Scenic construction and propmaking.	Liaison with SM and workshop. ■ Buy soft furnishings.	■ Choose hire furniture and scene painting.	Drawings for new props Alterations as necessary
Costume design and construction make up	Attend first rehearsal.	Check stock Measure all actors Buy fabrics Order wigs	Preliminary fittings Cutting and making	Keep in touch with rehearsals for new costume ideas Sort shoes
Lighting	Attend production meeting. Keep in contact rehearsals – SM/Director/Designer. Liaison with Director and Designer	Artwork and photography for projection ■ Construction special lighting affects.	■ Check stock.	Attend rehearsal and run through.
Sound	Attend production meeting. Basic provisional tape in rehearsal.	Research and planning. ■ Check stock and buy in tapes, effects records, etc. Meeting with director.	Prepare effects tapes. Sound meetings with director.	Record special effects. Record hire effects with actors. ■ Design sound rig. ■ Hire equipment.
Music	Singing rehearsals. Music rehearsals. →			Singers join main rehear
Choreography and fights	Dancing rehearsals. Fight rehearsals.		Hire weapons with SM.	Fights choreographed. Dancers join main rehea

Week 2	Day 7	Day 6	Day 5	Day 4	Day 3	Day 2	Day 1
...vite press to ...otocall.	Check Box. Engage FOH staff. ■ Ushers. ■ Sales. ■ Box Office.	Train FOH staff. Arrange FOH displays. Print programmes.				Photo call.	
...lish rehearsal. Fights in rehearsal. ...eet to discuss lighting. ...eet with sound dept, to ...eck final FX.	Introduce performance props.		Run through	Attend lighting and sound plotting sessions.	Attend technical rehearsal and give notes.	Photo call, dress rehearsal give notes.	Final dress rehearsal and gives notes.
...ake up production ...hedule. Arrange transport ...d staff for the get in/fit up ...d show staff.	Supervise get in and fit up as per production schedule	Continue fit up as per schedule (+ LX main rig).	Continue as per schedule. Possible fire inspection	Supervise schedule. (LX and sound plotting sessions).	Attend technical rehearsal.	Supervise technical work on stage. Attend dress rehearsal.	Supervise technical work on stage. Attend final dress rehearsal.
...range lighting designer to ...e an early run through. ...rector to listen to sound ...oc. Prepare setting lists ...d cue sheets.	Run rehearsals. Team attend run through. Finalize setting lists, cue sheets	Help fit up paint etc. Final props adjustments.	Team help move out of rehearsal rooms to venue.	Dress the set Set the props. Attend LX and sound plotting sessions.	Possible scene change rehearsal. Run technical rehearsal.	Run Dress rehearsal. Attend Director's note session.	Run final dress rehearsal.
...op meetings to check all ...ops. ...tend Lighting Discussion.	Fit up and painting as per production.	Continue fit up and painting as per production schedule.	Fit up and paint end texture as per schedule.	Attend lighting session and LX plotting. Dress the set.	Attend technical rehearsal.	Attend photo call. Attend dress rehearsal.	Technical work as necessary. Attend dress rehearsal.
...ccessories found/bought ...cond or final fittings	Check costumes, Check wigs arrived.	Get in for costumes. Costumes to dressing rooms.	Attend run through.	Attend run through Check make up.	Attend technical rehearsal. Check make up under lights.		
	Finalize copy lighting design. Preliminary rigging. Hired equipment arrives.	Lighting rigging.	Focusing of lighting.	Lighting session plotting.	Technical rehearsal.	Dress rehearsal. Attend notes sessions. Technical work on stage.	Final dress rehearsal. Technical work on stage.
...eparation of final tapes. Rehearse live sound ...xing – mini-tech. ...rector to hear tape.	Hired equipment arrives. Mini sound tech with orchestra.	Sound rigging.	Attend run through.	Sound plotting rework tapes.	Technical rehearsal. Rework tapes.	Dress rehearsal. Rework tapes. Attend notes session.	Final dress rehearsal. Attend notes session.
...sicians rehearse with ...und reinforcement if ...cessary.				Rehearsal for orchestra and cast.	Technical rehearsal, piano only.	Dress rehearsal with orchestra.	
...hts join main rehearsal.		Choreographer present as needed.					

The Run and Post Production

Function	The Run	Post Production
Administrator	Show reports to Director. FOH staff checks. Monitor sales. Liaise with Stage Manager.	File prompt script and production paperwork. Collect scripts. Pay accounts.
Director	Note running times. Director's notes to cast. Warnings and encouragement before performance. Keep contact with SM for problems.	File director's script. Compile report on production and contact list for cast or production team.
Production Manager	Work on budget accounts with Administration.	Arrange transport and staff for get-out. Supervise get-out and storage of any stock set. Supervise returns of hired/borrowed equipment. Final work on accounts with Administration
Stage Management	Run shows as per prompt script, running lists, etc. Check set, props, furniture settings. Supervise understudy rehearsals. Show reports.	Get out props, dressings and furniture. Supervise return of hired and borrowed items and stock to stores. Assemble prompt script and all lists, plots, etc. for the show and file with Administration.
Scenic Design and Construction		Sort out scenic stock to keep with Production Manager.
Lighting	Check performances crew present. Check equipment pre-performance. Run Show.	Dismantle and store lighting equipment. Return hired equipment. File lighting plot.
Sound	Check performances crew present. Check equipment pre-performance. Run Show.	Dismantle and store sound equipment. Store tapes and catalogue for future. Return hired equipment.
Costume Design		Cleaning and storage of costumes. File costume Bible.

THE TEAM

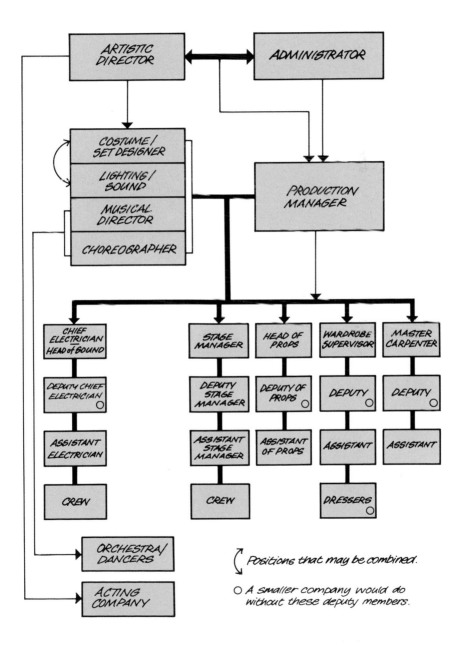

ARTISTIC DIRECTOR

ADMINISTRATOR

COSTUME / SET DESIGNER

LIGHTING / SOUND

MUSICAL DIRECTOR

CHOREOGRAPHER

PRODUCTION MANAGER

CHIEF ELECTRICIAN HEAD of SOUND

DEPUTY CHIEF ELECTRICIAN ○

ASSISTANT ELECTRICIAN

CREW

STAGE MANAGER

DEPUTY STAGE MANAGER

ASSISTANT STAGE MANAGER

CREW

HEAD OF PROPS

DEPUTY OF PROPS ○

ASSISTANT OF PROPS

WARDROBE SUPERVISOR

DEPUTY ○

ASSISTANT

DRESSERS ○

MASTER CARPENTER

DEPUTY ○

ASSISTANT

ORCHESTRA / DANCERS

ACTING COMPANY

⌠ Positions that may be combined.

○ A smaller company would do without these deputy members.

11

CHAPTER 2

SAFETY

A theatre can be a dangerous workplace. The work greatly involves electricity, which can kill – as can falling lanterns (lamps) and scenery – so proper safety measures must be adhered to at all times.

Those measures include legally enforceable local fire and safety regulations. They vary greatly from place to place, so contact your local safety officer and find out about the by-laws covering your theatre, which will include rules about placing lanterns in relation to the actors and audience. Never use naked flames without consulting the fire service first.

Every stage set has its own hazards, which the technician should recognize. Be alert to problems that may arise out of a given situation. Be aware. Keep informed.

AWARENESS

Whenever possible work with the power supply off, and never try to mend anything with it on. Disconnect electrical equipment from the power source whenever you can and see that it is all properly fused and earthed/grounded. If in any doubt ask a qualified electrician to inspect the equipment.

Overhaul lanterns and cables at least once a season and check them regularly for signs of wear and tear, especially when they are about to be used. Do not leave objects on top of ladders or where they can trip people up or jam doors.

Cable

Firmly tape down all loose cables, especially if they are hanging in doorways or where they may be caught. Cables should not be coiled too tightly or left in large piles; they generate heat if insufficiently ventilated, and can cause fires (see Rigging, page 46).

SAFE WORKING METHODS: USE PROPER PROCEDURES

Hard hats and safety harnesses should be available when needed, and protective industrial gloves should be worn by anyone handling hot lanterns.

The cry of 'HEADS' is the accepted way of telling people that an object has been dropped from above. If something is deliberately dropped from a height, the call 'Heads' is made calmly, with the location in which to be aware, e.g., 'Heads upstage left.'

Ladders

Ladders should always be footed to prevent slipping and checked for security before use. A-frame ladders should always be used fully open and never too close to the edge of the stage or platform. Never lean out from a ladder; move the ladder.

Lifting

Never lift heavy weights unaided, and when lifting, bend your legs and keep a straight back. Part of being aware is knowing your own limits and seeking information. See illustration and guideline.

Lifting lanterns

Check that everything on a lantern – including its safety chains – is secure before it is hauled up to be rigged or flown out. If sash or rope is used to haul a lantern out, be sure it can take the weight easily, and check during use that it is not being chafed dangerously thin as it runs over or through objects. When attaching a rope to a lantern do not simply slip a loop over the lantern's hook clamp; loop the rope under the yoke first (illustration).

KEEP INFORMED

Fire-fighting and first aid equipment must always be to hand and you must know where it is. Danger and advice notices should never be moved or obscured.
Be informed in other ways. Realize, for example, that theatre lanterns cannot just be plugged in anywhere. A socket you wish to use may be one of a pair already fully loaded. The lantern may have a low voltage bulb and have to be paired or transformed. Use this book to gather such knowledge but never hesitate to ask. In theatre work the learning is never over.

Hook clamp secured, the safety chain is then added.

Cable

Ladders

Lifting lanterns

Lifting

CHAPTER 3

LANTERNS

BASICS

The theatre lantern (lamp) is very simple and has scarcely changed in decades. It consists of a light source in a protective box with an opening at one end to let out light, which is strengthened by a reflector set behind the light source. Many variations on this simple design are produced by adding colour frames and lens systems to direct and refine the light.

The lantern is designed to be hung up or supported on a stand, and can be turned on both its vertical and horizontal axes and locked in place to point at the action.

Because of the heat they generate modern lanterns have protective shielding, ventilation and heat-protected adjusting knobs. Older types lack these features and heat-proof gloves are essential when operating them.

The various makes and types of lantern have different operating limits on which their manufacturers will advise. The most important information about any lantern is its *beam angle*, which gives the width of its beam and explains any variations involved.

From this you can work out how big a beam the lantern will produce at a given distance. The longer the distance the wider the beam. (See Lighting design, page 26.)

BULBS

Different lanterns have different shapes and are designed to take bulbs of particular types and power, so it is important to use the right bulb with any lantern. One designed for 1000-watt bulbs will overheat if fitted with a 2000-watt bulb. A smaller bulb in it – of, say, 500 watts – would also be ineffective as its element would not align properly with the reflector and lens system. Most lanterns allow fine adjustments to alignment to be made from outside with a screwdriver.

A new generation of quartz halogen bulbs is now replacing incandescent ones. They give a longer-lasting, stronger and whiter light but are more delicate than the traditional bulbs and must literally be handled with clean gloves. Dirt or grease on them shortens their life and can make them explode in use, though as lantern bulbs are not exposed exploding ones damage only the lantern interior.

Bulbs will operate only within a certain range of angles from the horizontal. Using one at angles other than those recommended shortens its life and can damage the lantern. This limits the rotation of lanterns. A lantern can be rotated from pointing straight down to pointing straight up, but if it goes over the top it is no longer within the correct working angles for the bulb. Also the colour gel frame may fall out! A lantern in such a range is said to be hung upside-down. Here again manufacturers recommendations should be observed.

LOW-VOLTAGE BULBS

Low-voltage bulbs are often used to produce sharp, bright beams from very small lanterns. They can be used on the conventional power supply if they are paired in series to make up the voltage. Thus ten 24-volt bulbs will add up to the British standard 240 volts. *Par bulbs* are examples of this (see Parcan, page 20).

FLOODS (PROJECTORS)

Theatre lanterns are defined by the various devices on them for controlling and shaping the light beams they produce. The simplest is the floodlight (projector).

The flood is as simple as the basic lantern described above. It has a bulb tray, a reflector and provision for fitting a colour frame, usually just a slot in front of the lantern's body. It has no devices to control or shape the light beam so the spread of light from a flood is increased only by moving it away from the stage.

Floodlights are widely used to provide large area washes of light, and because they do it so well many are manufactured for specific purposes, though generally the other lantern types are more flexible.

CYC FLOODS

These are floods for lighting a large vertical area like a backcloth or cyclorama (hence cyc). There is usually a row of them above and below the cyc, providing an even colour wash across the area. More rows of cyc floods are needed if more colours are wanted; new colours can be produced by mixing two or more colours (see colour section).

SPOTLIGHTS

Fitting a lens system to a basic lantern produces a spotlight. The lenses direct more light out of the lantern and allow it to be defined, shaped, and controlled to some degree. In all spotlights the size of the light beam can be changed by altering the distance between lens and bulb, usually by a sliding mechanism.

Two types of spotlight use two different types of lens to do two different jobs. The lenses are called *profile* and *Fresnel*, so the lanterns are the *profile* spot and the *Fresnel* spot.

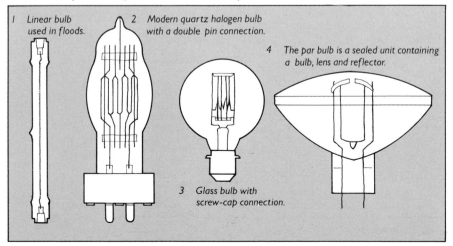

1 Linear bulb used in floods.

2 Modern quartz halogen bulb with a double pin connection.

3 Glass bulb with screw-cap connection.

4 The par bulb is a sealed unit containing a bulb, lens and reflector.

PROFILE SPOTS (LEKOS)

A profile lens will give a sharply defined image in outline of any object placed within its focal range, the area in which it can focus light. A profile spot (leko) is fitted with shutters, usually one on each of the lantern's four sides, which can be pushed into the light beam, shaping its appearance on stage. The lantern's (lamp's) focus allows the shutters' images to be defined through a range from very hard-edged to very soft. Sometimes a second set of shutters allows any one side of the beam to have a hard edge or a soft one as necessary.

On the top of the profile spot near the shutter set is a slot, the 'objective slot'. An opaque object dropped into it will be profiled like the shutters, and there is a range of such devices. *The mask* changes the shape and size of the beam by a fixed amount. *The iris* provides a variable-diameter circular beam. *The gobo* is a cut-out metal pattern whose image is projected on to the stage.

The profile spot does not permit a wide range of size variation. When used to profile a shutter it will give a hard edge at only one size, hence the masks, irises, and double shutter sets. But with two independent lens systems the profile spot becomes more flexible and works as a *zoom profile*, which allows a hard focus at various sizes.

Note: The profile spot, as most lanterns, needs its bulb to be properly aligned with the lens/reflector system. Many modern lanterns will provide an external knob for this.

USES

Because the profile spot (leko) projects shaped areas of light over a distance with sharp, hard-edged accuracy, it is ideal as the main light source on stage and for special areas.

THE FOLLOW SPOT

This can be a profile lantern with extra features or more than that (see Other lantern types, page 20).

Two examples of profile spots.

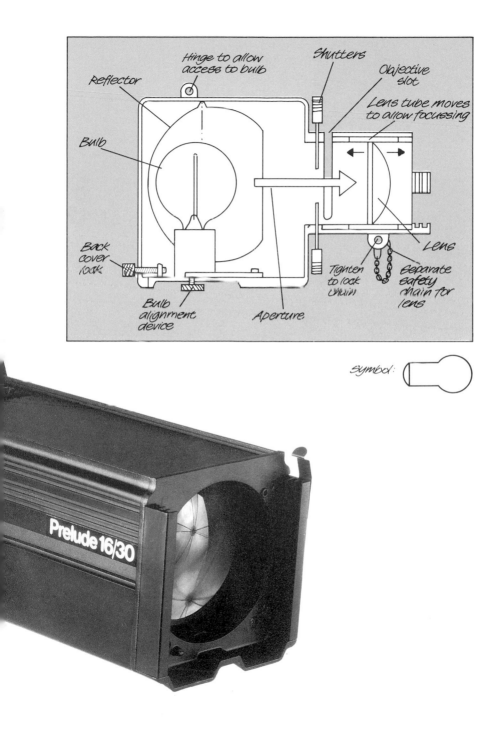

Reflector

Hinge to allow access to bulb

Shutters

Objective slot

Lens tube moves to allow focussing

Bulb

Back cover lock

Bulb alignment device

Aperture

Tighten to lock chain

Separate safety chain for lens

Lens

Symbol:

Prelude 16/30

THE FRESNEL SPOTLIGHT

The beam of the profile spotlight is relatively narrow. For lighting large areas of the stage the Fresnel spot is used.

The Fresnel lens was designed for use in lighthouses. Its inventor, Augustin Jean Fresnel, (1788-1827) took the very wide and thick lens needed for such a beam, sliced it up and put the sections one behind the other, reducing the width and bulk, but preserving the curve of the original. This does not make for a sharp focus so the Fresnel lacks many features of the profile lantern (lamp). It has no shutters or objective slot and it cannot 'profile' objects. It gives a soft-edged beam with large size variation. The only control of the light's shape is by externally fitted 'barn doors', which even so do not sharpen the edge of the beam.

Like the floodlight (projector) the Fresnel is used to create large washes of light, sometimes highly coloured, but as its size and shape can be altered it is preferable to the floodlight. Generally it produces less light than the profile spot for any bulb-rating so it is not usually used at any great distance from the stage.

The flood, profile ((leko) and Fresnel are the three most useful lanterns. Others are for specific jobs and so are less flexible.

Note also the description of a PC spot on page 20; this more effective lantern is fast becoming the preferred choice of lighting designers.

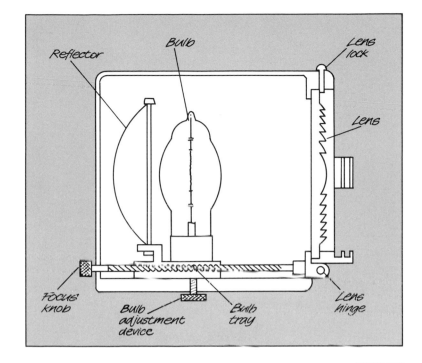

Reflector

Bulb

Lens lock

Lens

Focus knob

Bulb adjustment device

Bulb tray

Lens hinge

Symbol:

OTHER LANTERNS(LAMPS) THE BEAM LIGHT

This lantern (lamp) is designed to produce a beam as nearly parallel – i.e. with as narrow a 'spread' – as possible. It has been superseded in recent times by the Parcan.

THE PARCAN

The Parcan is simply a shell holding a Par lamp, a sealed bulb with fixed beam angle that produces a powerful, narrow beam like the beam light's. Par lamps come with Very Narrow, Narrow, Medium and Wide beam angles.

Originally developed for spectacles like rock concerts, Parcans are powerful light sources, excellent in groups or banks for creating curtains of light, especially in heavy colours. Their drawback as theatre lights is that they cannot be focused – i.e. their beams' shape and size cannot be changed. But Parcans are very effective in the rock-concert role they were designed for: making bold, bright banks of coloured light.

Many British lighting designers prefer the 110-volt American Par bulbs. On British 240-volt supply Parcans with these bulbs need to be coupled in series – i.e. 2 x 110v = 220v. A 110v bulb connected to a 240v supply will explode!

THE PC SPOT

This represents an attempt to improve the light output of the Fresnel spot by creating a hybrid. The 'PC' indicates the prism convex lens used in the lantern, which resembles the profile lens but is heavily frosted, making sharp shaping impossible. The PC does allow for large changes in its beam size and gives out a high proportion of its light. Its purpose is the same as the Fresnel's.

THE CSI FOLLOW SPOT

Follow spots can be variations on profile spots (lekos), with fitted irises and flip-over colour changers. Many are delicately balanced, with fitted sights and calibrated focus mechanisms for swift and accurate cueing. But in large theatres even the most powerful profile spot is too weak to act as solo follow spot. For this there is a low-voltage lantern whose light source is a bulb that arcs very high voltages between two rods. The light is bright and powerful, and very effective when focused on stage.

A CSI follow spot comes complete with transfomer; it must be lit before each performance and left running throughout, being dimmed mechanically with irises and shutters. The bulb cannot be lit quietly and must remain off for a certain time before it can be re-lit.

MOVING LANTERNS

There are now lanterns that can be programmed to move. The systems used vary from lanterns moved by motors, to rotatable mirrors placed in front of lanterns. The former have proved somewhat unreliable as their large motors, designed to cope with the heavy lanterns, can be difficult to maintain in a lighting rig. The latter have smaller motors doing a lighter job but are less flexible; their mirrors will reflect light only over a certain range.

VARI-LITES

These lanterns can be programmed to change not only their light level but also their direction, shape, colour – a choice of up to ninety – and size, and can be automatically loaded and unloaded with gobos. They come in profile and Fresnel versions but as yet can be only hired, not bought. Vari-lites perhaps hint at the theatre lighting of the future, but today they are still very expensive to use and confined to the big spectacular shows, like rock concerts, that can afford them.

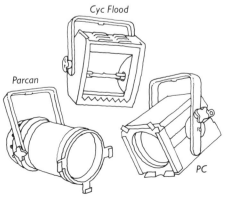

Cyc Flood

Parcan

PC

LANTERN SUMMARY CHART

LANTERN TYPE	GENERIC SYMBOL	NOTES
FLOOD	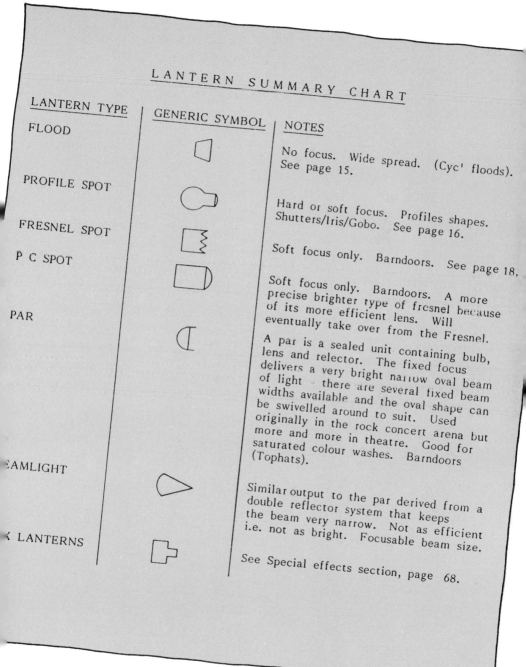	No focus. Wide spread. (Cyc' floods). See page 15.
PROFILE SPOT		Hard or soft focus. Profiles shapes. Shutters/Iris/Gobo. See page 16.
FRESNEL SPOT		Soft focus only. Barndoors. See page 18.
P C SPOT		Soft focus only. Barndoors. A more precise brighter type of fresnel because of its more efficient lens. Will eventually take over from the Fresnel.
PAR		A par is a sealed unit containing bulb, lens and relector. The fixed focus delivers a very bright narrow oval beam of light — there are several fixed beam widths available and the oval shape can be swivelled around to suit. Used originally in the rock concert arena but more and more in theatre. Good for saturated colour washes. Barndoors (Tophats).
ЕAMLIGHT		Similar output to the par derived from a double reflector system that keeps the beam very narrow. Not as efficient i.e. not as bright. Focusable beam size.
K LANTERNS		See Special effects section, page 68.

21

CHAPTER 4

CONTROLLING THE LIGHTS

Lanterns (lamps) can be plugged into the mains electricity supply of any building, **but most building installations will not have the supply to deal with many units. In a theatre, lanterns have to be used at varying levels of intensity and in different groups, so they are connected to a control board. Basically, this is just a battery of on/off switches, and even sophisticated units are still called switchboards. In order that the lanterns' light levels may be changed, they are usually connected to dimmers which are in turn connected to the 'remote' levers or buttons that form the switchboard. Each dimmer controls a lighting 'channel' or 'circuit'** There are two types of switchboard: **Manual and Computer. The many makes of each type, like the lanterns themselves, have very similar features, differing in layout rather than function.**

THE SIMPLE MANUAL SWITCHBOARD: DIMMERS

A single lantern or group of lanterns is plugged into sockets connected to a single dimmer. A 2000-watt dimmer will run four 500-watt lanterns – *not vice versa.*

FADERS

On a manual board each dimmer is controlled by a fader, a single remote sliding knob on the console. Each fader is numbered from one to ten with divisions between. A lighting state is created by adjusting the faders to different levels. The operator has notes of the levels required from each fader during any part of the performance, and sets these in order to change the lighting on the appropriate cues. Each cue signals a change of lighting arrangement to last through a segment of the play – an act, a scene, sometimes just a single second.

PRESETS AND MASTERS

The resetting of faders for each lighting cue would look very messy if it were seen on stage. To avoid this, each dimmer is controlled by two faders. The pairs of faders are arranged in two separate rows called *presets*. Only one preset operates the lighting state at any one time.

Each preset has a *master* fader that controls and overrides all of its other faders. When the master is set at zero the other faders on that preset will not work. The individual faders can be set at positions between zero and the level at which the master has been set. With the master set at full the faders can work over their whole range.

Presets allow the operator to set up a

lighting state in advance, unseen by the audience. Once set up the lighting works smoothly throughout the performance.

CROSSFADES

The lighting cues in a play can be successively set up on the preset not in use while the current cue, set up on the 'live' preset, is on stage. Small changes involving one or few faders can be faded neatly up or down on the live preset, but for a big one, involving several faders changing their levels, the operater changes from one preset to the other, using the masters. This change from one preset to another is called a crossfade, some lanterns being faded down and others faded up.

COMPLEX MANUAL SWITCHBOARDS

If equipped for more complicated functions a manual switchboard offers even greater flexibility. While two presets allow for smooth successive changes of lighting a board with more than two lets the operator set up lighting states even farther ahead.

The blackout fader

This allows manually timed dimming of all channels.

Grouping switches

With these each fader can be aligned with an A, B, or C group so that each preset can be split into three independently operated groups, creating three sub-master faders for each preset. This lets the operator set up a great many cues at one time. Without the need to reset the presets so frequently, the lighting can be worked by the master faders only.

The inhibit switch

This allows for the control of each channel – in all presets at once – to be taken over by a master inhibit fader that can override any preset levels. It is useful in emergencies, as when a lantern becomes faulty, obviating the need for a new adjustment to each pre-plotted lighting state.

Independent switches

These allow any fader to be freed from control by the master fader or the sub-masters. They are useful when lanterns must stay on throughout a performance or for other long periods, say as working lights. To prevent confusion the level of an independent fader can be set up only in one preset.

Timing devices

The timing of crossfades on manual switchboards is usually a matter of the operator's practised skill, but some manual boards have timing devices that allow crossfade speeds to be preset and crossfades to run at the touch of a button. On some manual boards the devices are very basic, and fast cues – 0-30 seconds – are better done by hand, but very long cues, sometimes up to 30 minutes, can be very difficult by hand, and then timing devices are very useful.

Left: a twelve-way, two-preset manual lighting board, with grouping and a simple timing device. Right: a manual lighting board with a twenty-four way facility.

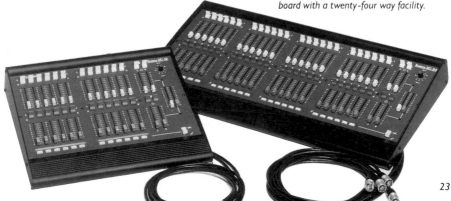

COMPUTER SWITCHBOARDS

Even a complex manual board eventually comes up against the problem of time. The number of accurate crossfades that can be achieved is governed by the type of board in use and the speed of the operator setting them up. An operator can work only so fast. Very complex cue sequences can take a long time to plot, and doing it in a hurry can be disastrous. Computer switchboards solve these problems.

A computer switchboard aims at the same result as a manual board – smooth and effective crossfading of lighting states – but it gives the operator more time to watch the action on stage rather than the workings of the board. It can memorize each lighting state and play it back over a pre-recorded time, fading different groups of lanterns up or down over very precise time settings. This is because it has the following set up:

Channel control
On a computer switchboard individual channels are called up and their levels set from a key pad. Groups of channels can be called up and set simultaneously. Levels can be set in many ways, using the key pad or a master dimmer – usually a wheel or touch-sensitive pad. Channels can also be flashed up or out for easy identification with a 'flash button'.

Memory recording
Once the channels are set, each lighting state is recorded and given a number. This part of the board is usually protected by a separate key – a memory lock – to avoid accidents when recording is not required.

Timers
The recorded memories can be set to include details on the speed of the fade. The time is usually set in two halves, one speed ('up time') dealing with lanterns (lamps) increasing their levels, the other ('down time') with those decreasing levels.

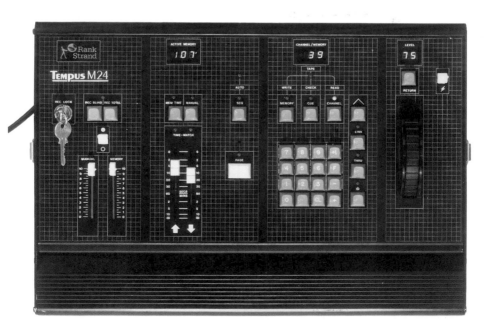

A modern memory board with 185 memories and 60+ circuits.

A hybrid board combining manual and memory features.

Playback

During performance the memorized lighting states are played back at the touch of a button. On older memory boards recorded memories were crossfaded into, a feature available on many modern boards as 'manual playback'.

The mimic

Information about the state of lighting on stage and available in other recorded memories is displayed on the lighting board on a 'mimic'. On older boards this is simply an indicator light for each channel combined with a meter showing lighting levels; on modern boards it is usually a sophisticated VDU display.

Like manual boards computer boards also have manual blackout switches and faders.

OTHER SWITCHBOARDS

The rock board

Like the Parcan this originated with rock concerts. It is was specially developed for 'playing' into concerts. It can be manual or computerized, with a 'keyboard' that lets the operator flash up many channels or groups of channels at the touch of a button to interact with live music.

The effects board

This board, which usually runs in parallel with a normal manual or computer board, is a means of running various automatic light sequences – a 'disco effect'. It may also include other electrical special effects – maroons (firecrackers), flares, pyrotechnics, streamers and so on. Many of the more expensive computer boards include effects panels.

The hybrid board

There are now switchboards with a bewildering mixture of the computer and manual set-ups. They are usually not very useful in the theatre. Be warned – too many options can simply confuse matters.

The preceeding pages have dealt with the lanterns (lamps) that are used in theatres for lighting and the machines that control them, this is all the information required to start discussing lighting design itself.

CHAPTER 5

LIGHTING DESIGN

Lighting design complements the work of everyone involved in mounting a theatre production. It heightens the audience's focus on an actor or a relevant part of the stage, and it steeps the unfolding tale on stage in exciting moods and atmospheres – which can be changed at the touch of a switch. There is almost no mood or effect, subtle or of great impact, that cannot be achieved with modern equipment. Every new theatre space, every new production offers new opportunities for lighting, and many exciting developments in the art are still to come.

Stage lighting has three main functions:

■ to make the actors clearly visible so that their expressions and emotions can be easily projected to the audience
■ to give actors and action a suitably dramatic appearance within the play's mood and setting
■ to complement and highlight the sets and costumes.

To walk into a big theatre and, for the first time, see the hundreds of lanterns (lamps) hung to light a show is to be convinced that theatre lighting design must be an enormously complex affair. Not so. The previous chapters show how very simple most of the equipment is. So is lighting design itself. A big

lighting rig takes time to hang and focus; the preparation must be well thought through; the designer's ideas must be clear. But however vast the scale of the event the principles of theatre lighting remain few and simple.

FOUR QUESTIONS

We have seen how lanterns and switchboards operate. Their use in a lighting design depends on four factors; four questions must be asked about each lantern:

■ where are we going to hang the lantern – that is, what *angle* of light are we using?
■ what amount of light – that is, what *level* – should we use the light at?
■ what gel are we going to use – that is, what *colour* do we want the light to be?
■ how shall we use the lantern – that is what *shape* is the beam of light to be?

To answer these questions we have to know what kind of lighting we want and what atmosphere we wish to create. When each question is answered for each lantern a design quickly takes shape.
Along with the equipment we have already discussed, the questions – on angle, level, colour and shape – are the designer's main tools. The next pages aim to show how they affect what we do with light.

LIGHTING ANGLES

When we light an actor or a set from a particular angle there are two factors to consider:

■ how does the angle of light illuminate the object or actor – that is, how well can they be seen, and with what consequent atmosphere/mood?

■ how do we justify the angle in terms of the real world? Does it represent sunlight? Electric light?

The second factor could be called the *motivation* behind the angle of light, and though it need not always be considered too literally it is very important in lighting design. Motivation is only touched upon here but we shall return to it when considering working with the text. Meanwhile the basic rules of light angles must be discovered. Let us start with those governing the first factor.

ONE ACTOR, ONE LIGHT

How does an actor or set look when lit from various angles? Imagine an actor at centre stage, surrounded by lanterns, all at head height. The plan shows the lighting rig. We will observe the actor from directly in front. We will disregard lantern (lamp) types, representing lanterns simply as light sources with arrows. This is what we see if we use each lantern in turn.

THE FOUR QUADRANTS

■ (A) From the front (frontlight) – a well-lit face but could it be more interesting? Against many other angles this is considered *flat lighting*. The actor's eyes are well lit – thought essential for communicating emotion

■ (B) from the side (sidelight) – too dramatic for general use but very interesting; half face, a look worth remembering

■ from the other side (sidelight) – obviously as above and a matter of personal opinion which side you prefer

■ (C) from behind (backlight) – not an angle for lighting actors' faces but an interesting effect.

THE FOUR DIAGONALS

■ (D) From downstage right – a good angle for lighting the face and eyes, and less flat than a frontlight

■ from downstage left – as above but the other side, again a personal choice

■ (E) from upstage right – an interesting variation on the backlight with a more specific light angle

■ from upstage left – like the above but from the opposite side

Obviously most theatre lanterns are not hung at head height. Let us look at the effects of various vertical light sources:

■ (X) from above – too steep to light the actor well but has a very dramatic effect

■ (Y) from above and in front – lights the actor and is more interesting than flat frontlight

■ from head height – this is, of course, the same as our initial source (A)

■ (Z) from the floor – a very dramatic, strange light source, the most unnatural.

The angles examined above are only a few of those available; many variations on them can be worked. They meet the two main requirements of stage lighting previously noted: making the actor clearly visible and giving him or her a dramatic setting. Some angles are good for lighting up the actor; others are less so but usable for dramatic effect. Combined light angles can manage to do both.

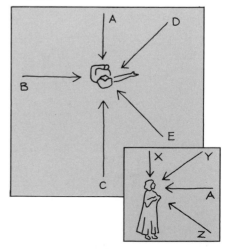

A

B

C

D

E

X

Y

Z

COMBINING THE ANGLES: LIGHTING THE ACTOR

The photographs show how lighting angles combine.

■ Left hand photograph – a light from in front of the actor, angled 45° from the horizontal, lights the face well, showing the eyes clearly. It is a natural light angle, neither too steep nor too flat.
■ Right hand photograph – a second light source in the same position on the actor's other side ensures that the whole face is covered.
■ Main photograph – a third light at 45° from the horizontal straight behind the actor, is only dramatic used alone, but combined with the other two it is a means of bringing the actor into the three dimensional world of the stage space. It outlines and adds depth to the figure, bringing it into relief.

LIGHTING THE SET

Light angles can be used to high-light a set separately from the actors. With sets, as with actors, flat light is not so good as angled light. A three-dimensional set looks best with light hitting it obliquely, the cast shadows emphasizing its dimensionality.

On the other hand, angled light on some painted surfaces may reveal textures inappropriate to what is painted on them, so they may be best lit flatly. The lighting designer must also consider any shadows *painted* on scenery. They must not contradict the real shadows.

Note in the main picture opposite how the folds and texture of the costume are highlighted by the lighting angles. This effect occurs with any textured surface, set, or costume.

LIGHTING CLOTHS AND GAUZES (SCRIMS)

Curtains look best in a side light, which throws attractive shadows into the folds. But painted cloths are best lit flat to show the picture clearly without revealing seams or levels of paint. Gauzes (scrims) lit from in front seem to be opaque, but when only the scene behind a fine gauze is lit, the gauze can disappear completely – a useful aid to transformation scenes. A gauze can also be hung in front of the whole stage – a popular ploy in opera – to give a scene a particular texture. In that event all light sources must be behind the gauze and a lot of side light used.

Hot lanterns (lamps) should never be placed close to a set, certainly never touching it. Do not rely on 'fire proofing' to prevent sets catching fire.

Top left: the actor lit with one lantern placed at a diagonal 45° from the front vertical axis, and 45° from the horizontal axis.

Top right: covering the whole face using two lanterns, placed one on each side – as above.

Main picture: the well-lit actor. He is lit using two lanterns as above plus a back light for added depth.

SUMMARY

An actor is best lit when:

1 The face and eyes are clearly visible, that is when the light angle is not too oblique. Steep top light casts too many obscuring shadows.
2 The light is at a realistic angle. Light from an unusual source – the ground, say – looks wrong.
3 The light gives the face character. Flat light is boring, shadows interesting.

■ flat lighting achieves 1 and 3 – character interrogatory
■ back lighting achieves 3 – character mysterious. But used with other angles it adds depth, makes an object more three dimensional
■ top lighting achieves only 3 – character dramatic. But it also adds depth when used with other angles
■ under lighting achieves only 3 – character macabre
■ steep-angled light achieves 2 and 3, but if too steep will not light the actor well enough to be seen. Character towards the dramatic
■ shallow-angled light achieves 2 and 3 – character towards the interrogatory. Also a good angle for sunsets and sunrises
■ between shallow and steep angles achieves 1, 2 and 3 – character realistic and interesting

To improve the lighting of the actor in the photographs above the light *levels* could be altered. Colour and plotting must also be considered. All these factors further enhance the effects of light angles (see page 28).

LIGHTING LEVELS

By adjusting light levels the stage picture can be further improved. One light source brighter than others is very effective and is said to give the scene a *key light*. In exterior scenes the motivation for a key would be the idea of sun- or moonlight. In interiors it might indicate sunlight through a window, or an indoor artificial light.

POINTS TO NOTE

Deciding how much light to use from a lantern (lamp) is only one part of *plotting*, balancing the lanterns in a lighting rig to create the stage picture required. It is a combination of all the factors discussed in this chapter.

Any colour gels to be used with lights must also figure in calculations of light levels. While colouring light they reduce its brightness.

Remember too that light from lanterns at less than full power becomes increasingly 'warm' as levels are lowered, a factor to be considered also when choosing colours (see next section, page 34).

The well-lit actor: all three lanterns are now coloured, giving the impression of directional sunlight. Various straw tints have been·used which also work well on the costume.

COLOURING THE LIGHT

In front of every lantern (lamp) is a space for a *gel frame*. Gels are translucent coloured plastic sheets. They are sold in rolls or pieces and are given names and numbers by the manufacturers for easy reference. The manufacturers also produce swatch books – books of gel samples – to help lighting designers choose their colours.

HOW GEL WORKS

White light is a mixture of all the colours. The colours are caused by the different wavelengths that make up visible light. This can be shown with a prism, which splits up the wavelengths and reveals many of the colours.

When white light from a theatre lantern passes through the gel only certain wavelengths, that is certain colours, are allowed through. The colours transmitted become the colour of the light that reaches the stage. Colours seem darker when the gel stops a greater percentage of the light passing through. As a part of the light stopped by the gel is converted into heat the darker gels get hotter in use, fade more quickly and need replacing more often than lighter ones.

HOW WE SEE COLOUR

Objects absorb certain light colours and reflect others. A red apple absorbs most light colours, reflecting only the red. We see only the colours reflected from an object. Thus coloured light can be used to enhance or dull objects, or change them completely. This is important to bear in mind when considering the lighting for an actor, set or costumes.

FITTING GELS

Lanterns take different sized gel frames so sheets of gel are cut to size for each lantern. Each colour then slots into a gel frame, or holder, that prevents it curling when it heats up. Gels come in many similar colours, so it is important to identify them accurately. Cut from a roll or sheet, they are usually marked with wax pencil.

POINTS TO NOTE

All gels are fireproof but become less so with age. They also fade and have to be replaced, darker colours fading first and fastest. The various manufacturers produce some colours in common, but a lighting designer will usually favour a particular range. Gels can be combined to make new colours.

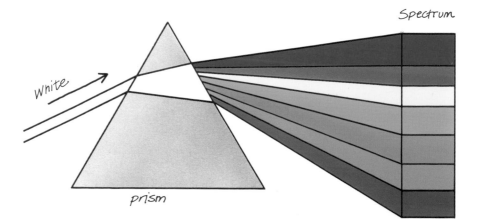

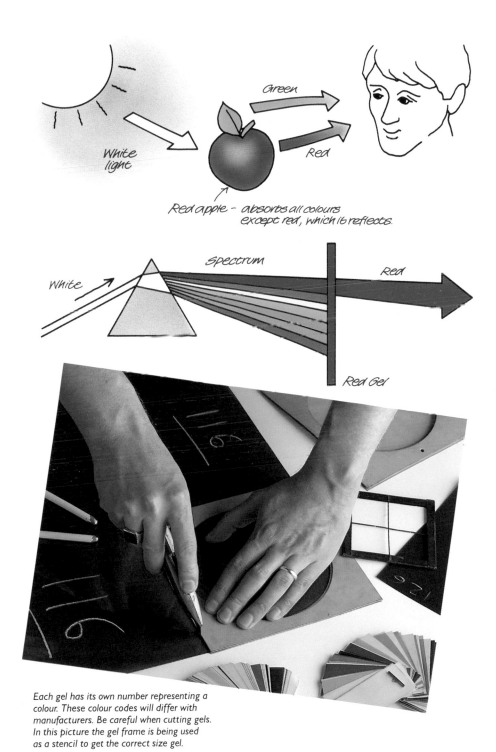

White light

Green

Red

Red apple – absorbs all colours except red, which it reflects.

White

Spectrum

Red

Red Gel

Each gel has its own number representing a colour. These colour codes will differ with manufacturers. Be careful when cutting gels. In this picture the gel frame is being used as a stencil to get the correct size gel.

USING COLOUR

Of all the aspects of stage lighting that decisions must be made about, colour is perhaps the most subjective. The following section aims to explain colour use in theatre lighting and to develop personal understanding.

THE PRIMARIES

White light can be split into three primary colours, *red, blue and green*. They can therefore be mixed together to make white light,; they can also be mixed in varying proportions to make all the other colours. But in theatre lighting the primaries are of limited use. To mix all of them three lanterns must be used, and as dark colours they drastically cut down the light. Using the primaries to make new colours is therefore usually a waste of resources. But this is less true when great colour flexibility is wanted and the darker colours particularly needed. Thus the three primaries are most often used in cyc-floods when the large area of a cyc has to be many different colours, as in light entertainment, vaudeville, pantomime and cabaret. Otherwise, colours are used more subtly.

COLOUR ON OBJECTS AND DARK COLOURS

Certain colours cancel each other out, and some complement others – especially darker colours. Remember that most colours are not pure. For example, purple has blue and red elements, and green may contain a lot of blue.

LIGHT COLOURS

Light colours are more often used to enhance the lighting of the actor and the stage picture. The light colours preserve the naturalism of the picture, which is why these *hues* and *tints*, are used more often than the dark colours. They simply warm or cool the scene, accentuating its mood without particularly registering as colours.

Remember also that light levels affect colour. Lanterns (lamps) produce a warmer light at lower levels. Allow for this when choosing the colour for a scene that is to be lit very dimly.

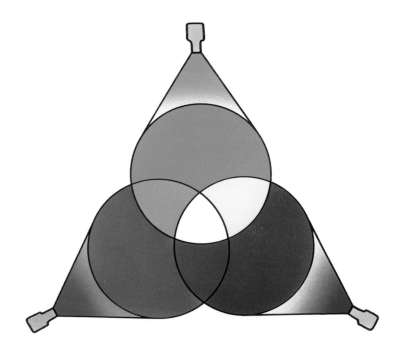

COLOUR CORRECTION

There are gels that alter the wavelength of light from one source to another. They are used in photography when natural light is mixed with artificial light but in the theatre they can be used as colours. They also allow alteration of light source colour 'temperatures', as when the light from a tungsten halogen bulb is changed to resemble daylight. The light produced from a CSI follow spot can also be realigned to other lanterns in the rig – e.g. CSI to a tungsten halogen. These gels can also be used to reduce the light output, useful when lanterns are paired on a circuit.

MIXING COLOUR

As light beams of different colours hit the stage the colours are inevitably mixed. Additional lanterns produce more light, adding to the mix, and this form of colour mixing is called *additional*. But new colours can also be produced by putting more than one gel into a single lantern. As this mixing method lets less light out of the lantern it is called *subtractive*. Both methods need experimenting with for the designer to decide where each is best used.

SPLIT COLOUR

Colour can also be split in a frame, with different effects in different lantern types. In the profile spot, depending on the focus, both colours can appear across the beam or to one side or the other. A four-way split diffuses the colour well. In a Fresnel the colours are located more on the sides of the beam but with no clear join. Split colour can be especially effective with gobos.
The colour slot is at the wrong focal point for the colour split to be defined clearly, so pictures cannot be drawn.

DIFFUSION GELS

Also called *frosts*, diffusion gels of various strengths are used to diffuse a beam. Though not colours they are part of the gel range. Various diffusion gels added to a lantern producing a hard-edged spot will have effects varying from softening the spot's edges to spreading the light all over the stage.

DIRECTIONAL DIFFUSION

This diffusion spreads the light along one axis only, which axis depending on how the gel is orientated in the lantern, and so how it is cut.

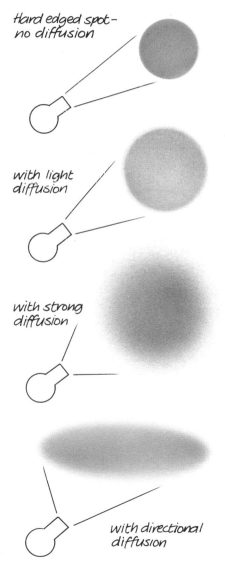

Hard edged spot – no diffusion

with light diffusion

with strong diffusion

with directional diffusion

SHAPING LIGHT

The ability to shape beams of light on a stage can be used to interesting effect. As seen above, the Fresnel lantern (lamp) allows only very soft-edged shaping; it's barndoors can spin before the lantern but do not move independently. The profile lantern's shutters move independently and can be focused to a hard edge, so it is much more useful for shaping light, and is often used for *specials*, where shape is frequently a factor. The photographs show the profile lantern's usefulness.

GOBOS

Projecting shapes from cut-out metal gobos is also a handy lighting tool. Gobos can be purchased from a catalogue or they can be cut by hand from any light, heat-resistant metal. Lithoplate, a printer's metal that can be cut with a sharp knife, is often used.

Cut lithoplate with care as the metal itself can be very sharp. Manufactured gobos, too, are very thin-edged. Remember also that gobos placed in front of strong light sources very quickly become extremely hot.

Gobos can be used to suggest many things and are especially effective if coloured. Most commonly used are the *window gobo* and the *leaf* or *break-up gobo*. These two show the two extremes of gobo technique.

The window gobo is one that is meant to be seen for what it is, light being shaped as it enters a window. These gobos are usually sharp-focused and very visible. They may be used in several lanterns to suggest further the reality of the wall in which the supposed windows exist. They can be rather obtrusive and should perhaps be used sparingly.

Leaf gobos, or break-ups, are in the class of gobos not usually meant to be seen as projected shapes but as part of the general lighting mood. Usually they are used in groups to suggest light streaming through trees, and are often softly focused and overlapped to cover the whole stage area. Though many gobos of this type appear in manufacturers' catalogues, a simple metal sheet with holes cut in it produces the effect extremely well. The manufacturers themselves produce many gobo types, simply called break-up gobos, for adding to atmospheric stage lighting without being too prescriptive. Split colour (see page 36) is especially effective in a break-up gobo.

Manufacturers also produce *composite gobos* which allow parts of an image to be projected from different lanterns and lined up as a single image on stage. This makes for a brighter image, one that can be used in parts and whose parts can be differently coloured. The best examples are perhaps the *stained-glass window gobo* of six different colours and the *flashing sign gobo*, which as well as having several colours can be made to flash on and off like a commercial sign.

Mesh gobos allow images to seem to float within each other without being connected. *Glass heat-resistant gobos* allow the image to be shaded.

Beam shuttered to sign

Brasserie

Beam shaped around actor

Beam shuttered to edge of stage

Beam shaped to make thin pencil beam across scenery

Gobos: standard (leaves), composite (church window), and tonal (clouds).

Window	Window	Leaf
Leaf	Tree	Break-up
Break-up	Graphic	Composite
Composite	Tonal	Tonal

A BASIC LIGHTING DESIGN?

The 'general cover'

There is no such thing as a basic lighting design! Each production needs a unique approach, starting with the text and involving director and stage designer. But sometimes a very diverse production calls for a 'general cover' of light on stage to which can be added special areas, colours and effects.

General cover is also useful when staging undramatic events that need only be seen clearly – speech days, visiting musical groups, acrobatic displays.

The stage area and lighting rig for general cover are shown here, the lanterns (lamps) either profiles or Fresnels. The front angles are 45°. Back and side lights give further definition and light, warm colours create a cheerful, unobtrusive atmosphere.

This set-up comes out of our knowledge of lanterns (page 8), lighting angles (page 28), lighting shape (page 38) and colour (page 36).

The number of lanterns is not arbitrary. The stage is divided into areas covered by different lanterns. Two factors affect the decision-making:

■ the desired angle of light – even if one lantern could adequately light the whole stage it would involve a huge range of angles crossing that stage

■ the beam angle of the lantern chosen – from the angle plus the distance from lantern to stage we can work out how much of the stage it will cover and so how many lanterns we will need (see Lighting, page 28).

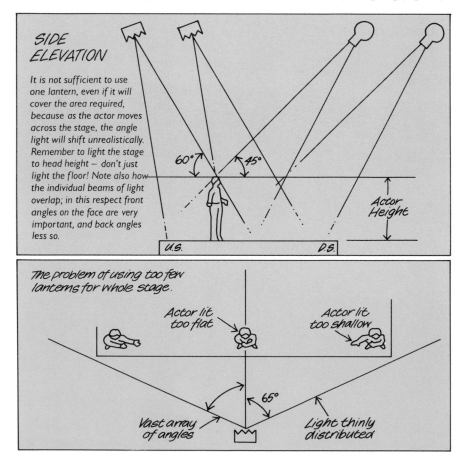

SIDE ELEVATION

It is not sufficient to use one lantern, even if it will cover the area required, because as the actor moves across the stage, the angle light will shift unrealistically. Remember to light the stage to head height – don't just light the floor! Note also how the individual beams of light overlap; in this respect front angles on the face are very important, and back angles less so.

60° 45°

Actor Height

U.S.   D.S.

The problem of using too few lanterns for whole stage.

Actor lit too flat   Actor lit too shallow

65°

Vast array of angles   Light thinly distributed

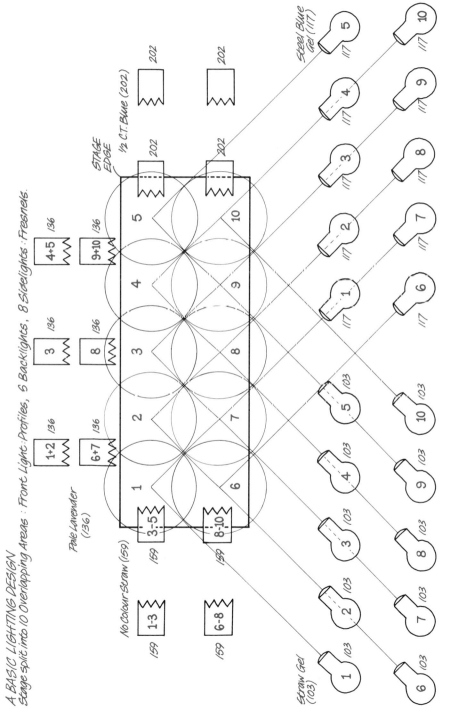

A BASIC LIGHTING DESIGN
Stage split into 10 Overlapping Areas : Front Light : Profiles, 6 Backlights, 8 Sidelights : Fresnels.

41

CHAPTER 6

PRE-PRODUCTION WORK

PRODUCTION STYLE.

Before a play can be produced it must be rethought, and related to the time and place in which it will be performed. This means finding a style for the production; as lighting designer you must understand that style fully before starting work. It is very important to have a good working relationship with both designer and director for they, more than anyone, decide the style. Early talks with them are as important as reading the text.

WORKING WITH THE TEXT

Lighting a production means approaching it with an open mind, seeking ways to enhance the material and 'bring it to life'. You must be selective and, finally, creative in your own right.

The text is your natural starting point. Read it thoroughly, perhaps more than once, and take notes. Lighting designers develop their own approaches to this, and should not feel in the least deterred by the prospect of close reading and annotating. Start by reading the text through quickly; be receptive to the play's pace and drama. Then read it a

second time, noting *all* the relevant details of time, place and atmosphere.

Though you may have to return to a text many times you must not become too 'text-bound'. An author, worrying too much about the appearance of a play, may fill a text with limiting instructions. These deny the concept of an original production style, so some of them may have to be ignored. Here is an example of text analysis, a page from Shakespeare's *Macbeth*.

WORKING WITH THE DIRECTOR

The director directs the technicians and actors in a relationship based on two-way communication of ideas. The technicians support the director with their know-how for realizing his or her ideas. As lighting designer you should promote this relationship, contributing to the production style out of a clear understanding of what the director and designer want.

All lighting ideas must be checked for the director's and designer's approval. A lighting rig can be a complex affair, and during the production week there is usually time for only minor changes. The director's word is final. Cost and time are usually the limitations here.

Lighting design notes on a production of Macbeth

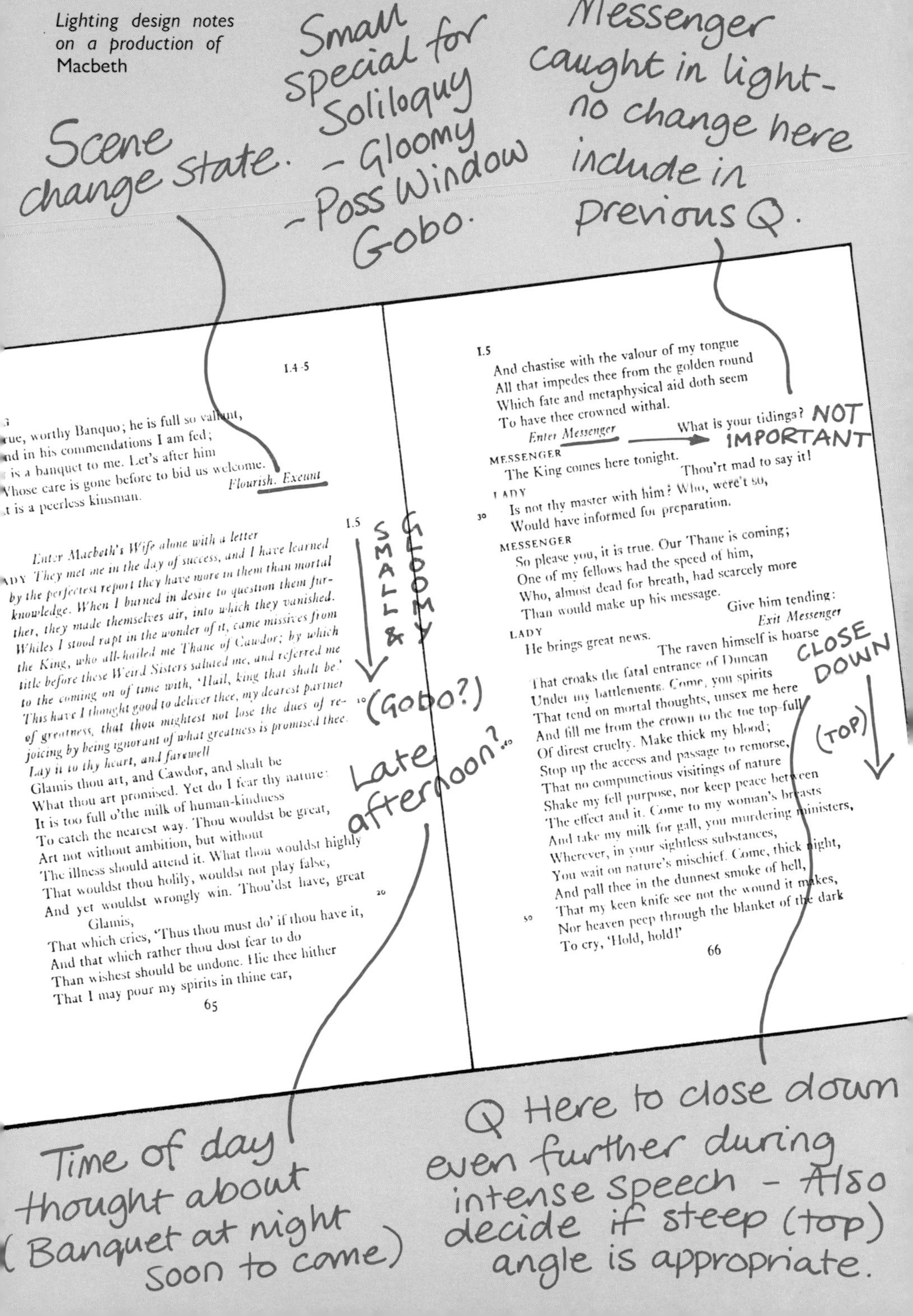

Scene change state.
Small special for Soliloquy – Gloomy – Poss Window Gobo.
Messenger caught in light – no change here include in previous Q.
I.4-5
…G
…rue, worthy Banquo; he is full so valiant,
…nd in his commendations I am fed;
… is a banquet to me. Let's after him
…Whose care is gone before to bid us welcome.
…t is a peerless kinsman.
Flourish. Exeunt
I.5
Enter Macbeth's Wife alone with a letter
…ADY They met me in the day of success, and I have learned by the perfectest report they have more in them than mortal knowledge. When I burned in desire to question them further, they made themselves air, into which they vanished. Whiles I stood rapt in the wonder of it, came missives from the King, who all-hailed me Thane of Cawdor; by which title before these Weird Sisters saluted me, and referred me to the coming on of time with, 'Hail, king that shalt be!' This have I thought good to deliver thee, my dearest partner of greatness, that thou mightest not lose the dues of rejoicing by being ignorant of what greatness is promised thee. Lay it to thy heart, and farewell
Glamis thou art, and Cawdor, and shalt be
What thou art promised. Yet do I fear thy nature:
It is too full o'the milk of human-kindness
To catch the nearest way. Thou wouldst be great,
Art not without ambition, but without
The illness should attend it. What thou wouldst highly
That wouldst thou holily, wouldst not play false,
And yet wouldst wrongly win. Thou'dst have, great Glamis,
That which cries, 'Thus thou must do' if thou have it,
And that which rather thou dost fear to do
Than wishest should be undone. Hie thee hither
That I may pour my spirits in thine ear,
65
SMALL & GLOOMY
(Gobo?)
Late afternoon?
I.5
And chastise with the valour of my tongue
All that impedes thee from the golden round
Which fate and metaphysical aid doth seem
To have thee crowned withal.
Enter Messenger
What is your tidings?
NOT IMPORTANT
MESSENGER
The King comes here tonight.
LADY
Thou'rt mad to say it!
Is not thy master with him? Who, were't so,
Would have informed for preparation.
MESSENGER
So please you, it is true. Our Thane is coming;
One of my fellows had the speed of him,
Who, almost dead for breath, had scarcely more
Than would make up his message.
LADY
Give him tending:
He brings great news.
Exit Messenger
The raven himself is hoarse
That croaks the fatal entrance of Duncan
Under my battlements. Come, you spirits
That tend on mortal thoughts, unsex me here
And fill me from the crown to the toe top-full
Of direst cruelty. Make thick my blood;
Stop up the access and passage to remorse,
That no compunctious visitings of nature
Shake my fell purpose, nor keep peace between
The effect and it. Come to my woman's breasts
And take my milk for gall, you murdering ministers,
Wherever, in your sightless substances,
You wait on nature's mischief. Come, thick night,
And pall thee in the dunnest smoke of hell,
That my keen knife see not the wound it makes,
Nor heaven peep through the blanket of the dark
To cry, 'Hold, hold!'
66
CLOSE DOWN
(TOP)
Time of day thought about (Banquet at night soon to come)
Q Here to close down even further during intense speech – Also decide if steep (top) angle is appropriate.

VIEWING THE MODEL

A good set designer will produce accurate plans of the set and a precise scale model. These will probably first be presented to the production team at the *production meeting*, usually before rehearsals start and well before you are ready to draw up a design. This may be the model's only appearance in one piece – carpenters, prop makers and set painters often take parts away to work with – so you must seize this chance of discussing the set with designer, director and others. The model is invaluable to the whole team, and a look at it is worth a hundred conversations. You can see at once the relationship of actors to set, and of pieces of set to each other – the placing of its parts and of the furniture, their shape, height, colour and so on. Here are some points to remember:

■ be tactful at the meeting. It may be the first time for the designer and director to present their ideas, and you will be in frequent contact with them during the production period, so tread carefully. Still, some questions are better asked here and now; later may be too late
■ write down or sketch anything that may be useful later
■ check that the model fully represents the set and is not still incomplete. Typical question: 'Will the floor actually be that colour?'

■ take nothing for granted. A set can be more than meets the eye. Typical question: 'Will the stage curtains be painted, as on the model, or of fabric?'
■ you can question points that the designer should have taken into account. The designer, too, is fallible. Typical question: 'Is it right for the top of the set to be invisible from the circle?'
■ check details that may limit what you can do, pointing out any that may affect what the director wants of your lighting. The designer *may* have allowed for them – *or may not*. Typical question: 'Those heavy curtains may interfere with our idea of streaming sunlight into the room. Have we a problem?'
■ check the designer's and director's concepts about the lighting. They could be less familiar with the stage space and working methods than you are. Typical questions: 'Are you happy about the lanterns near the top of the set?' or 'Do you mind seeing lanterns above the set?'

Lighting ideas can be tried out on the model, angles and colours beamed on to it experimentally. This is often done quite crudely with torches or flexible desk lamps, but it can prompt valuable ideas and stimulate thinking. It can also be useful in testing ideas that have been used on the finished paper design – if the model is still available then.

Drawing up the lighting design.
Lantern symbols are drawn carefully onto a
scale representation of the theatre/set.

Stencils represent specific manufacturers,
lanterns (generic symbols could also be
used).

Text is still very much in use but the
lighting designer is also referring to a
summary of his notes.

PAPERWORK

The drawing shows the extent of paperwork for a typical lighting design. Some will be done by juniors or the chief electrician, but you must check it all. From the full design shown here an experienced lighting crew could begin to rig, circuit and colour the lanterns (lamps).

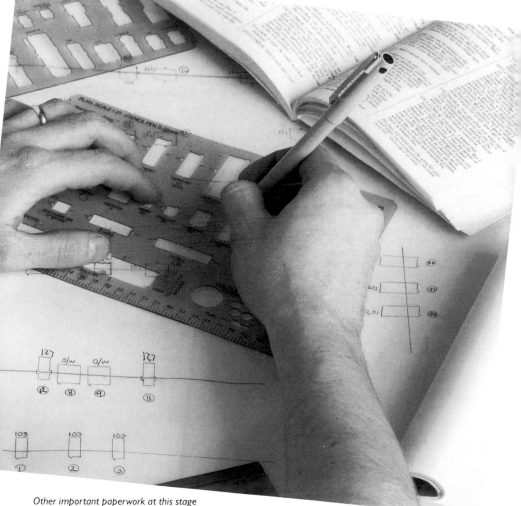

Other important paperwork at this stage
includes an equipment list, and a circuit
plan of the theatre.

CHAPTER 7

WORKING IN THE THEATRE

Putting a lighting design into a theatre is called rigging. The method described below has proved effective over the years, is fairly error-proof and enables others to understand your work in your absence.

A well-rigged theatre is tidier, safer (loose cables can be dangerous) and time-saving (fault-finding is easier). Be sure to read the safety section before your first attempt at rigging.

LIGHTING BARS

These can be counter-weighted or winched, each working individually. Some are wired internally as part of the permanent installation; others must be cabled up. In either case cable will run from the bar back to the dimmers.

This cable is known as *tripe*. Be sure that the tripe from a bar being moved is free to manoeuvre safely.

A fixed rigged network of bars is called a *lighting grid*. A short suspended bar is called a *trapeze*. A number of short bars hung as a vertical grid is called a *ladder*.

Lanterns (lamps) are hung on bars by *hook clamps* of various types. Check that these are locked firmly on to their bars and that safety chains provide extra security.

LIGHTING STANDS

Lanterns can also be supported on *lighting stands*, attached by *spigots* instead of hook clamps. A *T-bar* allows more than one lantern to be supported on a single stand.

Make sure that lanterns transferred to stands are *not rigged upside-down*.

BOOM ARMS

Lanterns can also be rigged on vertical lighting bars, called *booms*, fixed to walls or other parts of the set. This is done with *boom arms*.

GETTING UP TO THE BAR

High bars can be reached by ladders or scaffolding towers of the light Speedy Frame or Zip Up type but more often in theatres a telescopic platform on wheels is used.

HANDLING A TALLESCOPE

Always use outriggers. *Always* use brakes. *The person on top* is in charge of directing movement. *Do not lean out*; have the 'scope moved.

HANGING LANTERNS

The rigging method is the same whether you hang lanterns on a bar lowered to the floor, or on a fixed bar at height, though the latter is slower. Following information from the lighting design plan, you proceed as follows:

■ hang each lantern in place, lock the clamp hook and secure the safety chain

- point the lantern roughly where it should be pointing. This will give you a good idea of problems ahead. You may have to rethink if things are too cramped – or even impossible. It also helps when you focus
- if colours are ready put them into the lanterns
- plug each lantern into the cable. When plugged directly into permanent sockets the socket numbers must be checked against the lighting plan (see Plugging in, below)
- as a good safety precaution check also the power phase, which should be marked (see next section).

PHASING

Theatres need a large power supply to operate fully. Electricity, in AC form, is generated in *phases*. Usually a single phase is used for each separate part of a building's requirements – one phase for lighting, one

for wall sockets, and so on. If the theatre's lighting needs are big, more than one phase is used. Each phase of electricity carries the voltage and amperage expected at a normal socket, so two or more phases are that much more dangerous.

At the UK voltage a two-phase electric shock would almost certainly kill. The following rules *must* be applied:

- cable each lighting bar to *one phase only*
- do *not* cross-phase lanterns (lamps) that are close together
- check that lanterns hung on conductive material (that is, a metal work set) are *all on the same phase*
- arrange that *no one* can touch two lanterns on different phases at the same time
- as a general rule see that lanterns on different phases are at least two metres or yards away from each other.

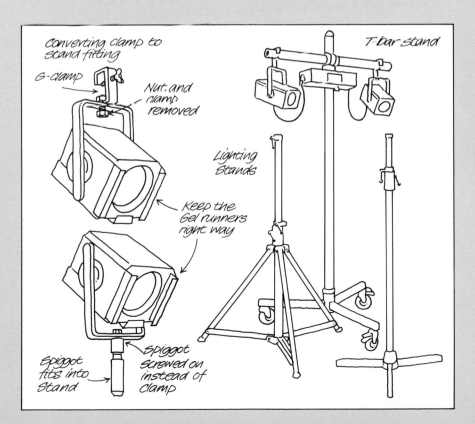

Converting clamp to stand fitting

G-clamp

Nut and clamp removed

Keep the Gel runners right way

Spiggot fits into stand

Spiggot screwed on instead of clamp

T-bar stand

Lighting stands

CABLING

The cables are plugged into groups of sockets, which should be clearly numbered. Phasing too, where appropriate, should be indicated (see above). A lighting bar that is not pre-wired has to be cabled, and this is best done when all lanterns (lamps) are on the bar. The lighting plan tells the rigger which way the cable must run to plug in. Sometimes cable has to be run off in both directions, in which case it is best treated as two separate bars. Cabling procedure is as follows:

■ start at the opposite end of the bar to where the cable will run
■ make sure your cable is long enough – cables can be joined up but it makes fault-finding harder
■ tie or tape the socket end of the cable on to the bar beside the lantern (lamp), and on the side farthest from the way the cable will run. This lets the cable, if it is accidentally pulled, to slide along the bar to the hook clamp rather than dislocate the lantern; it also leaves some slack near the lantern in case it needs to be moved slightly
■ plug in the lantern (often forgotten!)
■ take the cable along to the next lantern, add the next cable and tie or tape the two together
■ tape up any cable that sags between the lanterns
■ plug each cable into a live socket. This 'hot line', for checking that lantern and cable are both working, is especially useful on a bar that is to be flown out. Changing either

bulb or cable is much easier now than later
■ mark each plug top with the socket number shown on the plan. This helps in sorting out a tripe if the bar is to be flown out and plugged in later. (It also helps later if a number of cables are accidentally pulled out, when it could take ages to trace the cable to each lantern.) The best way is to stick black tape on each plug top and write the number on it in white wax pencil (easy to see in the dark)
■ when the cabling is done check the bar visually to make sure all is well before moving on.

With practice these procedures become second nature, and a rig can go up or be put in very speedily.

PLUGGING IN AND PATCHING

The lanterns and cables are plugged into marked sockets. The sockets may run straight back to the dimmers, or go first to a *patching* system, which allows greater flexibility and shorter cable runs by having many lighting sockets throughout the building, indeed more sockets than can actually be supplied with power. The sockets are run back to a patching panel where they terminate as plugs. Those that are to be used are then plugged into sockets connected to the dimmers. Some productions even require a 'running patch' – changes of patching during the performance. This may be cued along with the lighting changes themselves.

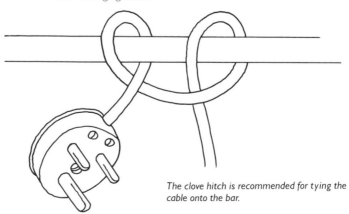

The clove hitch is recommended for tying the cable onto the bar.

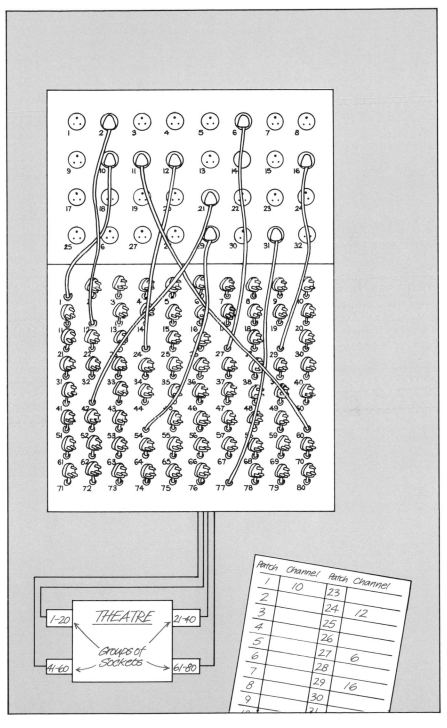

FOCUSING

The best size for a focusing team is four or five; the lighting designer on the floor, instructing; the switchboard operator turning on the lanterns (lamps); the electrician (the focuser) focusing each lantern; and one or two people to steady and move the ladder and generally run errands. Focusing is better done on a quiet stage so that the lighting designer can concentrate. Each lantern is brought up in semi-blackout so that it can be clearly seen. This is the procedure:

■ the board operator fades each lantern up before putting out the previous one, so as not to black out the stage, which can be dangerous. If the focuser is not yet at a new lantern, it can be brought up to a low level (about 30 per cent power) to keep it cool and to check that it is working. Lanterns are usually focused at 90 per cent power, as the bulbs are very prone to blow if moved when full on

■ the focuser needs an adjustable spanner or wrench for lanterns stuck in place. If force is needed to move a lantern it should be turned off first, as any violent movement will blow the bulb

■ a lantern should be focused as small as possible – 'spotted down'- so that you can see the centre of the beam clearly

■ you must remember precisely where each lantern is to go and what its function is. Check, for instance, that it covers actors when they lie or jump as well as when they stand

■ centre the beam in its correct position by standing where its centre needs to go, or by verbal instructions

■ once the beam is centred, the lantern should be locked firmly in position

■ facing away from the light, so as not to be blinded, and using your shadow as indicator, give further *clear* instructions to the focuser: 'up, down, left, right, smaller, bigger, left shutter to here' and so on. Some lighting designers use hand signals to indicate direction, size and shape – which can be particularly useful if focusing must be done against noise.

■ when satisfied with its focus you may need to check a light against others with which it is to be used, for example to check general cover overlaps, or to see that specials are in line or symmetrical.

PROBLEMS

This is a nerve-racking time for you. Only now can you see if the ideas that look good on paper actually work on stage.

If a lantern is not doing what was expected of it a decision must be made; change it for another? move it? add a new one? leave it for the time being? The decision will rest on many factors, not least being the pressure to keep to schedule. If problems can be solved quickly and easily, deal with them at once. Alternatively, at the end of a session, analyse the extent of larger problems, prioritize them, and deal with them accordingly.

Time is set aside during the production week that follows for technical work on stage, and though it is ideal to go into the lighting session or first dress rehearsal fully prepared it cannot always be. A typical production schedule is shown on pages 8-9.

Clearly it is important that *most* of the thinking behind the paper design has been correct! Time for correcting mistakes is very scarce once the stage must be shared.

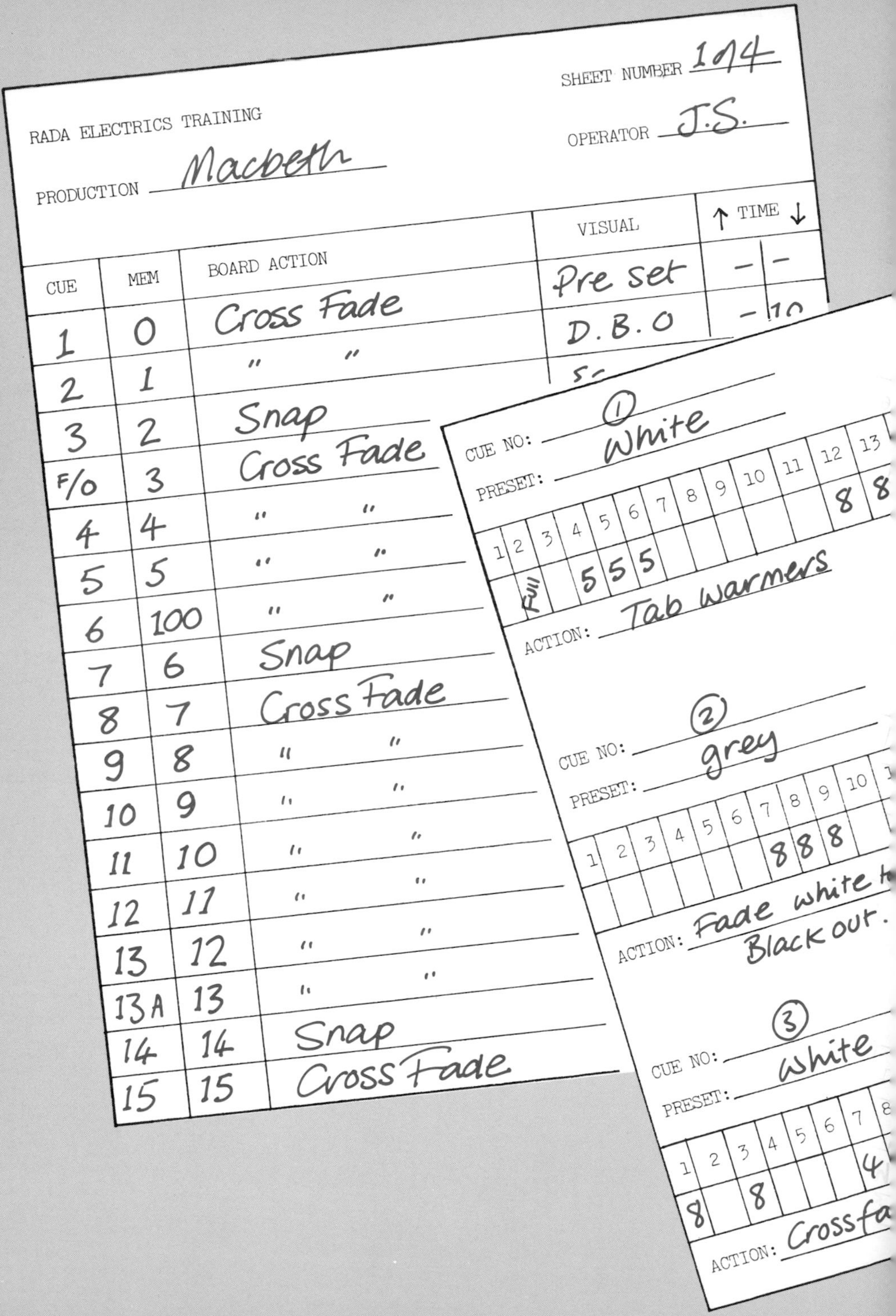

RADA ELECTRICS TRAINING

SHEET NUMBER 104

OPERATOR J.S.

PRODUCTION _Macbeth_

CUE	MEM	BOARD ACTION	VISUAL	↑ TIME ↓
			Pre set	— | —
1	0	Cross Fade	D.B.O	— | 10
2	1	" "	S—	
3	2	Snap		
F/o	3	Cross Fade		
4	4	" "		
5	5	" "		
6	100	" "		
7	6	Snap		
8	7	Cross Fade		
9	8	" "		
10	9	" "		
11	10	" "		
12	11	" "		
13	12	" "		
13 A	13	" "		
14	14	Snap		
15	15	Cross Fade		

CUE NO: ① White

PRESET:

1	2	3	4	5	6	7	8	9	10	11	12	13
											8	8

| Full | 5 | 5 | 5 | | |

ACTION: Tab warmers

CUE NO: ② grey

PRESET:

1	2	3	4	5	6	7	8	9	10	1
							8	8	8	

ACTION: Fade white to Black out.

CUE NO: ③ white

PRESET:

1	2	3	4	5	6	7
8						4

ACTION: Cross fa

16	17	18	19	20	21	22	23	24	25	26	27	28	29	30	31	32	33	34	35	36
									Full	Full					3				5	

AFTER CUE: _____

TIME: _____

14	15	16	17	18	19	20	21	22	23	24	25	26	27	28	29	30	31	32	33	34	35	36
5	5	5				8	7	6						Full	Full							

AFTER CUE: Re-set white

TIME: 10 seconds down / 5 seconds up

up main state.

11	12	13	14	15	16	17	18	19	20	21	22	23	24	25	26	27	28	29	30	31	32	33	34
			5	3	3				4	3	3						5	5					

AFTER CUE: Re...

TIME: 10 seconds

hite state nightime.

Lighting cue sheets. A record is made of each circuit's individual level in the appropriate box.

THE LIGHTING SESSION

At this session the lighting cues are created and *plotted* on to the switchboard by the operator. You are showing the director and stage designer the visual realization of your design for the first time. The lighting is now given its overall shape, and several other things happen:

■ the deputy stage manager (DSM) enters all cues in *the book*, a master copy of the text with all lighting cues marked in it. You must check that it is done properly, noting the cue numbers
■ the other switchboard operator sets up every cue as instructed and writes down any appropriate information (cue sheets are shown on pages 54-55). In lighting sessions 'walkers' often stand in on stage for the actors. They must be employed usefully. Remember that they are not wearing the right costumes. Also much time can be wasted getting an even light in places where the actors will not go.

At this stage the lighting designer must still respond flexibly to the needs of the production and its director. Here are some pointers:

■ you may wish to show the director the blocks of lighting you plan to use, and have them pre-set to speed up the session. But do not allow the switchboard operator to show any lighting before you are ready. Good effects are worth saving, and once shown one, a director may want to use it immediately, everywhere!
■ do not plot lantern levels at full. Leave something in reserve – 60-70 per cent power is a good starting point
■ there is no need yet to define each cue completely. Instead take time to get the cues' main intentions clear. Fine tuning – especially of timings – can be done later, when the actors are on stage in their correct places, that is during the technical rehearsal
■ do not present a cue as complete all at once. Even if there has been prior time for some plotting, the director may want a say in it, and will understand more readily what has gone into each one by seeing it built up in stages

■ use the operator to show your director cue sequences if necessary.
* Take coherent notes of jobs to be done – for example alterations needed – and of the cues themselves.

THE PRODUCTION PERIOD

For the rest of the production period you should continue refining the lighting.

THE TECHNICAL REHEARSAL

This is expressly to rehearse all the production's technical aspects and to sort out any technical snags. The switchboard operator, cued by the DSM, rehearses the lighting cues, and they are fitted in with the rest of the production. Anybody with problems – for example the switchboard operator – informs the production manager or stage manager, who will have them sorted out. The lighting designer can stop the rehearsal to re-run lighting sequences and iron out problems. Progress is usually slow during the 'tech', as time is taken to replot cues.
After a tech you will probably have further opportunities for minor changes to rig, etc.

DRESS REHEARSALS

These are full try-outs of the production and cannot be interrupted. With care, replotting can be quietly carried out – at the discretion of the DSM and switchboard operator. Be careful here; putting the switchboard operator under too much pressure now can cause mistakes; on memory switchboards memories could be lost! Note-taking is preferable.
After each dress rehearsal you should have a chance to get back on stage for as long as necessary to perfect focusing and make other changes. Time on stage has to be negotiated with the production or stage manager. When time is short, be sure that jobs are done in order of priority.
Though there will be time for further lighting changes before the first night, it is better if work proceeds on the understanding that the final 'dress', at least, is viewed by the whole production team as the perfected show.

AFTER THE FIRST NIGHT

If possible you should return to the production now and then during the run to see that no sloppy working has crept in. The technical crew can get bored with their nightly jobs. Check also that no lanterns have blown or slipped.

THE SHOW ROUTINE

The procedure before each performance should be as follows:

- an hour before the 'half' – that is 95 minutes before curtain up – the rig is checked for blown lamps, follow spots are lined up, etc
- at the 'half' – 35 minutes before curtain up – the tab warmers or presets are put on stage and the switchboard made ready. The technicians sign in in a book controlled and checked by stage management
- at the 'beginners (places) call' – 5 minutes before curtain up – the technicians take their places
- during the performance, technicians can leave their positions only by permission of the DSM.

CHAPTER 8

LIGHTING DESIGN EXAMPLES

THE BOX SET

The box set follows the convention that the stage is a normal room, the wall nearest to the audience – the 'fourth wall' – being removed. It generally calls for naturalistic lighting. It can seem very easy, but may prove very difficult. The flat wall surfaces, particularly, show up blemishes that on a floor surface would cause no problems. This production of The Odd Couple, **by Neil Simon, calls for a basic** general cover for early evening and night, linked with a sunset. The diagram shows how this is achieved.

■ the general cover has been flattened slightly at the sides because of the building's nature, but as none of the audience can sit past the edge of the stage, no actor will seem to have a face shadowed on this side as a result. So that the angles of light do not change too markedly from sides to centre they have been flattened out towards the stage edges, a common 'compromise', especially in proscenium theatres. This arrangement of FOH lanterns (anti-pros) is called *fanning*

■ to cope with both evening and night light a second cover of lanterns (lamps) in different colours could have been added front of house, but this is costly in equipment and time. It may need only one side of the cover doubled up by using a neutral colour on the other, suitable for both night and day interiors. One could even use all the FOH in neutrals and double up the other lanterns' angles to get the necessary change in colour. Here the top light is doubled, involving a lot fewer lanterns

■ powerful Fresnel top lights cover a larger area of stage than the FOH profiles. FOH angles are important – they light faces; the top light can be allowed a much greater angle

■ proper side light is impossible on such a set (some clever ones have concealed side-lighting gaps in the walls). Here a steep side angle is used

■ back light is also impossible because of shadow from the back wall, so top light is the compromise. This happens also if the designer wants to avoid light spilling off the stage, yet still light actors who stand on the stage's front edge

■ cyc lanterns in day, night and sunset colours are used for the sky backcloth, on which small bulbs convey the lights of apartments in other buildings. A ground row hides the lanterns on the floor

■ so that the light is not cut off as actors walk through the doors the area immediately behind them is lit

■ parcans provide the light coming through the windows, their colouring and angles successively conveying day, sunset and night, and lanterns outside produce the on-off glow of nearby neon lights

■ a bank of parcans could carry the idea of sunset light through the window down stage. From the auditorium, the difference in angle will not be noticeable.

■ cloud gobos are projected on to the cyc, fluffy white ones for day, long pink ones for sunset. A moon gobo features in the night scenes

■ the set has several working household lanterns, or 'practicals', cabled to dimmers and backed by theatre lanterns within the rig

■ behind the upstage window is the effect of a neon sign outside the apartment.

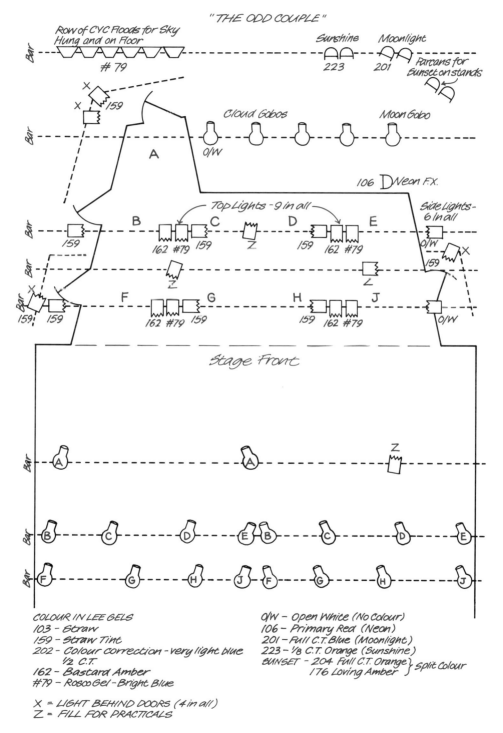

"THE ODD COUPLE"

Row of CYC Floods for Sky
Hung and on Floor
#79

Sunshine 223
Moonlight 201
Parcans for Sunset on stands

Bar

X 159
X

A

Cloud Gobos
O/W

Moon Gobo

106 D Neon F.X.

Bar

Top Lights - 9 in all

Side Lights - 6 in all

Bar   159   B   C   D   E   O/W
162 #79 159   Z   159 162 #79   159   X

Bar   Z   Z   159
159 159   F   G   H   J   O/W
162 #79 159   159 162 #79

Stage Front

Bar   A   A   Z

Bar   B   C   D   E B   C   D   E

Bar   F   G   H   J F   G   H   J

COLOUR IN LEE GELS
103 - Straw
159 - Straw Tint
202 - Colour Correction - very light blue ½ C.T.
162 - Bastard Amber
#79 - Rosco Gel - Bright Blue

X = LIGHT BEHIND DOORS (4 in all)
Z = FILL FOR PRACTICALS

O/W - Open White (No Colour)
106 - Primary Red (Neon)
201 - Full C.T. Blue (Moonlight)
223 - ⅛ C.T. Orange (Sunshine)
SUNSET - 204 Full C.T. Orange } Split Colour
176 Loving Amber }

57

THE THRUST STAGE

A thrust stage is viewed from three sides, though usually most of the audience is in front. To light such a stage properly a general cover must be extended to include a good 45° front light cover from the side. If the audience is evenly spread round three sides it may as well be lit like in-the-round (see page 60).

Thrust stages have their own problems. Here is how a production of Shakespeare's *Macbeth* was dealt with:

■ general light cover extends only as far as the action, and here the up-stage setting sees none, functioning only as a three-dimensional backcloth. The front cover is angled at 45°

■ on such a deep stage, strong back light is possible though it is steepened near the stage front to stop it spilling off too much. Back light is angled as three-quarter back-light

■ the general cover is meant to be used in its separate areas, or in blocks, for various scenes in the play, so the areas covered by it are not all the same size

■ splitting up the 'general' area also dictates that there be a central area. Downstage centre is a powerful place to act from, and often has to be isolated. If there is doubt it is as well to make the general cover an odd number of stage areas to incorporate this

■ extra lanterns are added to the isolated parts of the 'general', appropriately keyed or coloured for the scenes they will light

■ various 'specials' are needed; a window gobo when Lady Macbeth is first seen, reading Macbeth's letter by a window's light; a follow spot subtly used for Lady Macbeth wandering with the candle; a narrow parcan for the appearance of Banquo's Ghost; small soft-edged specials to isolate actors for soliloquies and so on. The nature of the play is such that its mood dictates the angles of specials, so they follow no discernible logic on paper

■ the setting needs at least two lanterns for each special so that the whole audience can see the actors involved. On a proscenium stage a single front angle is enough

■ specials on the upstage area must be very bright because it is so far from some of the audience

■ the three-dimensional backcloth must be well lit to be clearly seen so far from the audience

■ the white floor will pick up colour well and can be a major production feature, especially with so little setting down stage, hence the three top light colour covers. Colour is a major part of the different scenes

■ the white floor will also show shapes well, and a gobo cover has been added in weird break-ups that can double for leaf gobos with other elements of the rig – for example the 'general' – or appear on their own as part of the witches and ghost scenes. The gobo cover angle is opposite the back light so that they can be used together

■ a smoke machine will much enhance the atmosphere. Smoke shows the light beams, heightening the mystery and weirdness needed at some points (see page 72)

■ lanterns on the front-of-stage floor will play a weird up-light on the action and cast big shadows of the action.

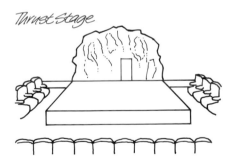

Thrust Stage

Possible general covers

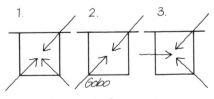

Main variations only

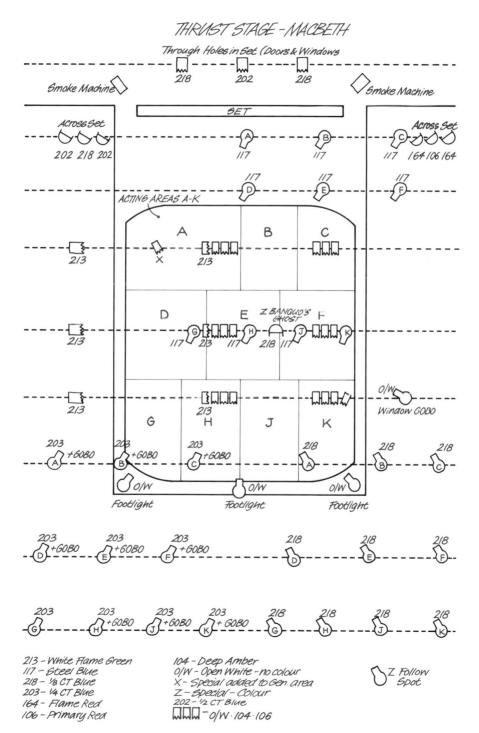

THRUST STAGE - MACBETH

Through Holes in Set (Doors & Windows)

218   202   218

Smoke Machine   Smoke Machine

SET

Across Set   Across Set

202 218 202   A   B   C   164 106 164
                  117   117   117

        117   117
ACTING AREAS A-K   D   E   F   117

213   A   B   C

                X
213   213

        D   E Z BANQUO'S   F
                      GHOST
213   G   H   J   K
            117 213 117 218 117

                                        O/W
213   213   213   Window GOBO

        G   H   J   K

203   203   203   218
+GOBO   +GOBO   +GOBO   218 218
  A   B   C   A   B   C

            O/W   O/W   O/W
        Footlight   Footlight   Footlight

203   203   203   218   218   218
+GOBO   +GOBO   +GOBO
  D   E   F   D   E   F

203   203   203   203   218   218   218   218
+GOBO   +GOBO   +GOBO
  G   H   J   K   G   H   J   K

213 – White Flame Green   104 – Deep Amber   Z Follow
117 – Steel Blue   O/W – Open White – no colour   Spot
218 – 1/8 CT Blue   X – Special added to Gen. area
203 – 1/4 CT Blue   Z – Special – Colour
164 – Flame Red   202 – 1/2 CT Blue
106 – Primary Red   ⊓⊓⊓ – O/W · 104 · 106

59

STAGING IN THE ROUND

Because in-the-round theatre has seating all round the stage, care must be taken not to light into the audience. A general cover can be made from two 45° covers facing each other, as the 45° angle splits a circle neatly into four, but this can be a costly use of lanterns (lamps). To avoid this, the angle is widened out to 60°, providing three main light angles on each stage area. The axis of these angles is placed to give the main part of each seating block an interesting set of front and back light angles, particularly the block that would otherwise have had only a flat angle. The main points about this design for a production of Arthur Miller's *The Crucible* are:

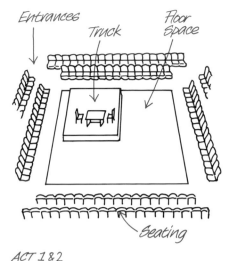

Entrances Truck Floor Space

Seating

- with three angles in use, one person's back light becomes someone else's front light. Added lanterns to highlight the actors may be unnecessary; one can over-light! Remember too that the action can never look the same from all the seating at one time, but take time to check on how each stage looks from each part of the auditorium
- the staging changes for each act but the lighting areas overlap usefully, the first two acts completely covering the third act stage area. If the area's lights are soft-focused discrepancies will be lost
- the first act is lit in a fairly ordinary way but the courtroom is provided with very strong top light in open white – i.e. no colour – to convey a gladiatorial, interrogatory feeling
- specials highlight important parts of the coutroom like the witness box
- it was decided that window gobos of big courtroom-type windows would weaken the setting's claustrophobic nature, but a window gobo and lanterns backing up the light from the window are used in the first act, where the oppressive drama has yet to develop.

ACT 1 & 2
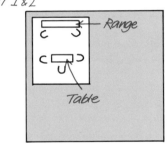
Range
Table

ACT 3
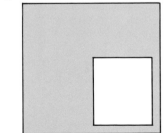

ACT 4
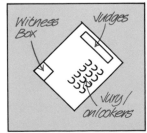
Witness Box
Judges
Jury / onlookers

IN THE ROUND
"THE CRUCIBLE"

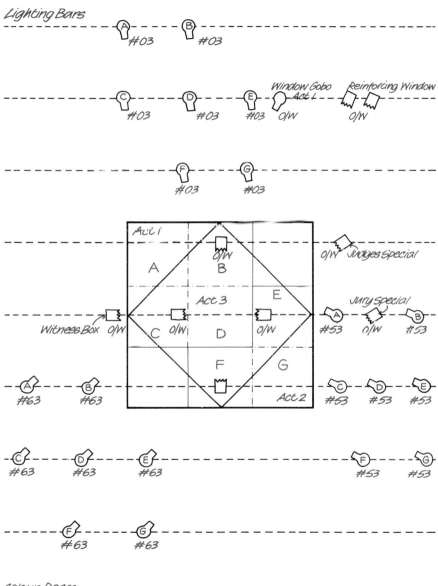

Lighting Bars

A #03   B #03

C #03   D #03   E #03   Window Gobo Act I ○/W   Reinforcing Window ○/W

F #03   G #03

Act I

A   B ○/W   ○/W Judges Special

E
Act 3   Jury Special

Witness Box ○/W   C   ○/W   D   ○/W   A #53   ○/W   B #53

F   G   Act 2

A #63   B #63   C #53   D #53   E #53

C #63   D #63   E #63   F #53   G #53

F #63   G #63

Colour ROSCO
63 – Steel Blue
03 – Dark Bastard Amber
53 – Pale Lavender
O/W – No Colour

61

LIGHTING OTHER THEATRE FORMS

You should look closely at traditional ideas about lighting various types of theatre. Just as each piece must find its own production style, so must the popular approaches to all kinds of theatre be carefully reassessed. They may be popular for all the wrong reasons, and seem like cliches in a new context. Tread carefully!

TRAGEDY AND COMEDY

There are no traditional styles for lighting the two extremes of drama except that lighter, brighter colours and less oppressive angles suit comedy, and their opposites suit tragedy.

DANCE

In a 'straight theatre' the actor's face is our prime consideration; in dance the performer's whole figure must be clearly visible, isolated from its surroundings, so most light comes from the side. To light the figure fully and evenly, place your lanterns (lamps) at foot, knee, waist and head height. Lanterns placed in the wings are easily accessible for colour and focus changes during the performance. But take care that they do not obstruct dancers who leave the stage at speed. Back light can also usefully silhouette the figure, and the front light can be less bright and shallow than in drama; seeing the dancers' eyes is rarely a priority.

Because the stage must be generally bare for most dance pieces, smoke is often used to show up the light beams as a structure on stage. Some companies fill the behind-curtain area with a light mist just before curtain up.

MUSICALS

In musicals visual spectacle may be more important than plot – if there is one! – so the lighting is usually very colourful. Pinks and purples replace the softer, less intrusive straws and light blues of the straight drama, and some very strong colours are also used. Some lighting designers achieve a colourful stage by colouring into the shadows cast by other lanterns.

Costumes are an important part of the spectacle so the lighting designer should pay special attention to them when choosing colours. Sharp follow spots ('spotlights') may be needed for some numbers, and footlights may lend the show a traditional feeling.

Dance numbers may call for attention and the stage setting for many exciting 'prac ticals'. Naked bulbs round the scenery may add to the 'theatre' feeling of a piece set in the theatre world. *Chasers, mirrorballs,* and other special effects may be needed. More serious pieces will demand a mixture of styles, as in *Cabaret,* where the seedy glamour of the cabaret is set against oppressive scenes of violence in the real world outside.

OPERA

Traditionally opera is lit in parts, with no general cover. The set, often a massive structure, is lit very dramatically, as befits the scale of the piece. The stars are isolated in follow spots, often quite unsubtly. Most soloists sing their arias down stage centre – to see the conductor and to be seen to advantage – so there is no reason for follow spotting, but the tradition lingers on, even though modern equipment allows subtle lighting of any part of the stage. The chorus is usually lit as part of the set, because operatic producers want them heard rather than seen. Chorus performers notoriously sing better than they act, and are best left in the shadows! The ballet sequences in some operas require special treatment.

REVUE

Revue can share many features of the musical – colour, footlights, chasing lights, practicals, attention to costumes, follow spots, smoke for atmosphere, and many lighting cues.

PERIOD PIECES

A piece purporting to be set in a time before electric light must be faked. Footlights will work, as they are used in the era of oil lighting and were the nearest a light source could be to an actor when the projection of light was not far advanced. The footlight tradition carried right into the use of gas and electricity, and has only recently been dropped from straight drama. Real candles are illegal in most theatres and anyhow are very hard to control. Electric substitute candles can be effective (see page 64) and can be backed up with theatre lanterns. Textured gobos can give an authentic period look or theatrical style if used as general cover or as part of one.

Stage setting from the English National Opera production of The Makropoulos Case, *by Janáček; lighting design by Nick Chelton.*

CHAPTER 9

'PRACTICALS'

These are stage features, rather than usual theatre equipment. Light-producing household objects – for example, electric fires, television sets, refrigerators – can house lanterns or bulbs and be dressed to seem real. A small red LED powered from a battery can make appliances like irons and radios look more as if they are working on stage.

Take care when adapting and building even simple circuits. Many plastic light fittings are wired with two-core cable, no earth being needed; for the stage an earth should be added. Bigger objects are used on stage than at home, and may come in contact with the fittings.

LAMPS AND LIGHT FITTINGS

Obvious specials are lamps that would be found in the room that a set represents. All of these can be wired to theatre dimmers, though dimmers may not work too well with very small loads or very low bulb wattages. In such a case the practical can be wired in parallel with a second (concealed) lantern to share the load.

When light switches are part of a set or practical they should actually work when possible. It is difficult to cue lighting to coincide with the moving of a switch, though if

any lanterns come on they may have to be cued. Then it is better if the actor faces the switching and waits for the light before taking his or her hand from the switch.

Even at low wattage bare bulbs can be dazzling. Low-hung ceiling lights can make problems with the other lighting. Negotiate with the designer about hanging them higher or even cutting them out.

CANDLES AND FLAME TORCHES

Naked flames are usually forbidden in a theatre, but there are some effective fake electric candles. Some flicker more naturally than others, and some move too. You may have to dress lanterns carefully to obscure further any 'electric look', while any wiring must be concealed. Transparent plastic-covered cable helps to hide wiring that cannot be run inside lanterns – e.g. on solid silver candelabra.

Lanterns to be carried can have hidden batteries, but may have to be switched off in long scenes to conserve the power. A switch-over device can enable a lantern to be carried on, glowing under its battery power, put down and then discreetly powered from the mains supply via the switchboard. The actor seems to turn up the lantern, which is actually faded up from the board to a higher level than the battery could manage. Batteries must be checked for every performance.

Manufactured electric candle effect units

The simplest method of making a candle using
a battery, bulb holder, bulb and cellophane.

FIRES

Real fire, like any naked flame, is usually forbidden on stage, but stoves and fires are cheaply and easily faked. Lanterns can be built into such practicals, coloured appropriately and randomly chased from the switchboard, but this is wasteful of valuable circuits, while many chasers will not give the required randomness. A simpler solution uses starters from fluorescent light fittings wired to ordinary bulbs. The starters flicker the bulbs continually in random patterns. Suitably dressed, they can be very effective, especially combined with smoke. Electric fires can be 'cheated' with red lamps, especially small strip lights.

LIGHT BOXES

Signs can be easily built, as shown. To prevent the bulb elements being seen the bulbs are put behind the front of the sign and reflected off the back of the box. The sign is coloured with sheets of gel.

A special kind of light box is the *moon box*, meant to look like the moon. Such a box may have diffusion gel in front as well as a colour, and is usually flown on fine wires behind a gauze or cloth.

STARS

Small bulbs can be flown upstage as stars, if the wires are unnoticed. White Christmas tree lights can be effective. Star cloths can be made, hired or bought with the bulbs and wires hidden in the material. Silver paper can be hung on threads and side lit to look quite effective as stars twinkling as they move. *Fibre optics* are increasingly used for these and other effects (see page 71)

FLUORESCENT LIGHTS

Fluorescent light can be effective when a harsh cold light is wanted. The tubes come in many shades of white and can be coloured by being wrapped in gel. They will not dim on standard theatre dimmers but must be switched on and used at full capacity (they also flicker as they are lit). But you can hire or buy a special fluorescent dimmer. A unit can help to fade more than one light. Careful shielding of fluorescent lights is often necessary because of their big spilling potential.

NEON

Neon lighting is very expensive, because each piece of tubing must be specially commissioned and powered, but there are cheaper alternatives, the *light box* described above being one. There is also a type of fluorescent tubing that glows like neon when lit by UV light, though not so brightly, and the UV light source must be very close.

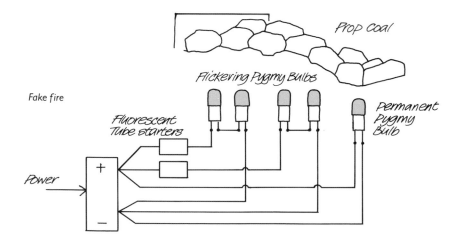

Prop coal

Flickering Pygmy Bulbs

Fake fire

Fluorescent Tube starters

Power

Permanent Pygmy Bulb

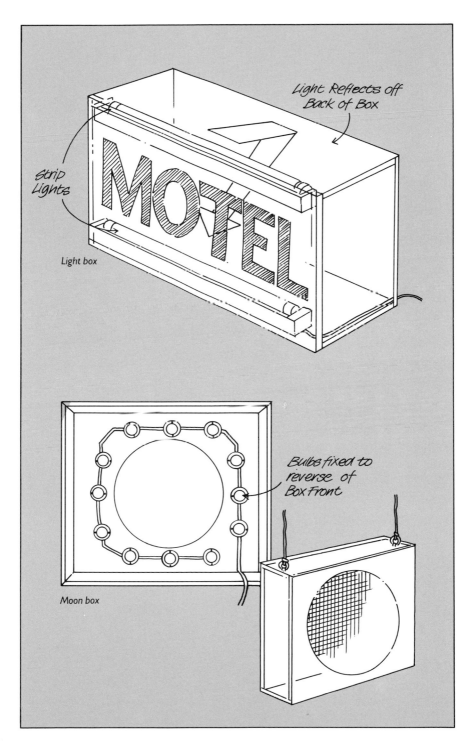

Light Reflects off
Back of Box

Strip
Lights

Light box

Bulbs fixed to
reverse of
Box Front

Moon box

CHAPTER 10

SPECIAL EFFECTS

Many of these effects can be used in combination in order to get the desired result for a particular scene.

CHASERS

Many modern switchboards are equipped with *chasers*, units that will flash lanterns, (lamps) or groups of lanterns, on and off. They can be programmed to vary the pattern and speed of on/off flashing for each group or lantern. If used carefully, overlapping flashing lights can give the effect of movement.

PROJECTED EFFECTS GOBOS

Of the many simple effects that can be fitted to theatre lanterns, the most obvious is the *gobo*, which projects a prefabricated pattern. Popular gobos include projections of leaves, lightning, windows, skyscapes, clouds and many other designs. Gobos can be purchased, or are easily made (see page 38).

COLOUR CHANGERS

Other projected effects include colour changers, in wheel form or semaphore. The wheel revolves in front of the lantern. It has five compartments that can hold gels of different colours. The rotation speed is fixed. The semaphore usually holds four colours. Unlike the wheel it allows more

than one colour to be in place at once – or none. Both types of colour changer work by remote control, though the wheel can also just revolve continually when powered. Several lanterns in a rig can be fitted with colour changers cabled to change simultaneously or separately.

FLICKER WHEELS (KK WHEELS)

These rotate in front of lanterns to give an effect of movement. Depending on the lanterns' focus the movement seems rough or smooth. Properly coloured and used with a gobo they can convey the light cast by moving flames, light bouncing off water, psychedelia and so on.

EFFECTS PROJECTOR

This is a special lantern for projecting moving effects on stage. It contains a full-colour slide on a continuous wheel. Though expensive to buy, a projector can be hired fairly cheaply. Effects obtainable include clouds, (fleecy, stormy, etc), fire, moving water (rippling, running, lapping, etc), rains, snow, and psychedelic patterns. Two of these effects projected on top of each other can give a very realistic three-dimensional effect.

Check that a projector has the correct lens for the size of image you want. Masks can be fitted to these lanterns to cut off unwanted spill (they have no shutters.)

Light curtain: This unit is designed to hold a number of par lanterns which if directed vertically downwards will give the appearance of a solid wall of light, (the use of smoke helps this effect enormously).

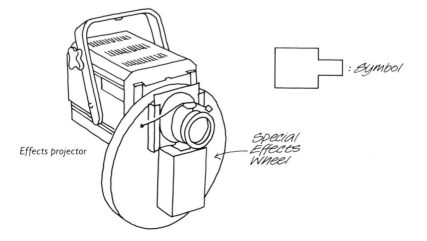

Effects projector

Special Effects Wheel

: Symbol

OTHER MOVING EFFECTS: THE RIPPLE TANK

This actually contains water from which light is reflected on to the stage. Handle with care.

THE RIPPLE TUBE

This consists of a tubular bulb placed behind a revolving metal tube with slots cut in it. It produces an effect of light hitting the tops of waves. It works well on clothes for sea-scapes and beaches.

MIRROR BALL

This ball, faceted with small mirrors, gives the well-known ballroom effect but can be effective elsewhere – for example, stationary, with coloured lights chased on to it and the ball itself out of sight.

Mirror ball

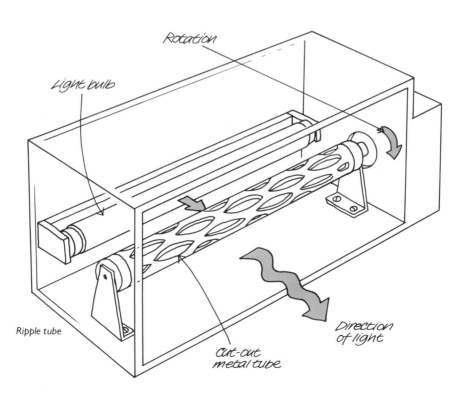

Ripple tube

Rotation

Light bulb

Cut-out metal tube

Direction of light

STROBES

The strobe flashes a very clean light at fast regular intervals, and if used alone it can seem to put the action into slow motion. Its speed can be changed and it can be successfully used for such other effects as camera flashes, lightning and underground trains passing.

Strobes can be used for only a short duration (local rules differ), and notice must be given to the audience if one is to be used. Certain strobe speeds are usually illegal as they can provoke epileptic attacks and muscle spasms, including starting a birth.

PHOTO FLOODS

The ordinary photo flash can be used as a lightning flash. Some hire firms offer a number of hangable flash bulbs in floodlight housings, operated from one unit.

FIBRE OPTICS

The main feature of fibre optics is that the fibres will carry light from a remote source which can be a normal theatre lantern. Fibre optics can be very effective in a stage set, though they must be used in large quantities to produce large, bright lights. They can now be purchased cheaply, and used in combination with colour changers and chasers.

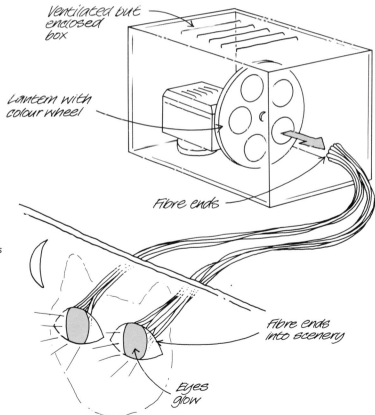

Ventilated but enclosed box

Lantern with colour wheel

Fibre ends

Fibre optics

Fibre ends into scenery

Eyes glow

OTHER STAGE MACHINES: BUBBLE MACHINES

These machines are large versions of the child's bubble-blowing toy, incorporating fans and rotating bubble makers.

SMOKE MACHINES

Note that these machines have parts that get very hot in use.

Smoke is used not only to represent obvious events like fires. It can subtly and effectively give texture to the stage, revealing the beams of light from lanterns to show colour in mid air and add to the shape of the set.

Smoke machines for the stage come in many types and sizes, generally not very well made (follow the instructions rigorously). Because of this they are better hired than bought. The 'smoke' is vapour produced by heating special liquids and is released under pressure. It is harmless and the modern liquid is totally non-irritating.

Smoke can be hard to control and must be well tech'd. Some local authorities have rules about the amount of smoke used in productions and allowed in the auditorium. Smoke usually rises, depending on the ambient temperature. For an effect of smoke along the ground dry ice can be effective.

DRY ICE MACHINES

Dry ice is solid carbon dioxide. It is very cold and must be handled with care as it burns naked skin. Vapour is produced by putting the dry ice into water. The warmer the water the faster the vapour is made. It takes a great deal of dry ice to cover a stage, it can be expensive and it is hard to store. The vapour is harmless but local authorities usually restrict its use, as in very large amounts it could cause suffocation.

PYROTECHNICS

Take care with these effects. They are fireworks for the theatre.

Most local authorities will wish to see the pyrotechnics set off as in the production

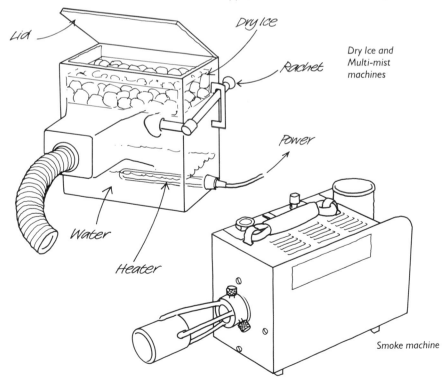

Lid

Dry Ice

Rachet

Dry Ice and Multi-mist machines

Power

Water

Heater

Smoke machine

before granting a licence for it or allowing it to procede. Use only proper theatre pyros' and follow the manufacturers' instructions. They are best fired by professional firing mechanisms, as shown. Here are the rules for using pyro's with this equipment.

SAFETY RULES FOR PYROTECHNICS

■ firing boxes must have two switches, one lockable. The person loading a pyro must check that the device is switched off and must have the key while loading, the key being fitted only just before firing
■ pyros should be stored in locked metal cabinets; stored explosives should be kept to a minimum
■ they should be transferred from the store to the place of detonation in a lockable metal box
■ people handling them should not smoke while doing so
■ a pyro should be loaded at the last possible moment – but not in a hurry
■ the person detonating the pyro should be the nearest one to the effect – at the regulation distance – and have a clear view
■ during the technical rehearsal do not set the pyro before the moment of its first use. Wait until the tech reaches the moment of detonation and then stop the tech. Explain

the effect to actors who will share the stage with it, then show it in operation. Only then work it into the production itself.

There are three types of pyrotechnic: *maroons (firecrackers)*, *flashes* and *streamers*.

MAROONS (FIRECRACKERS)

These have the effect of explosions. They come in various sizes exploding with various booms, cracks and bangs.
Explode maroons (firecrackers) inside a regulation cast (that is, seamless) bomb tank, compartmentalized if more than one is to be set off. Put a mesh over the tank to stop small bits of maroon flying out, but be sure it is not too fine to let the blast escape properly. Empty the tank before each use.

FLASHES

These come in various types – genie flashes, coloured flashes, coloured fires, coloured showers, etc – and can be very effective.

STREAMERS

These are detonated by a pyro charge. They include glitter and, most spectacularly, confetti cannons

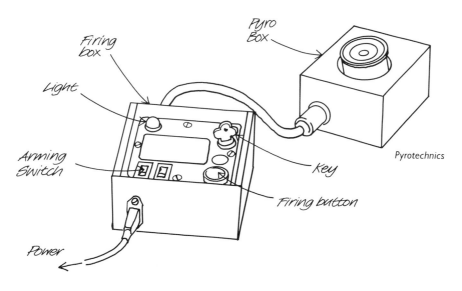

Firing box

Light

Arming Switch

Power

Pyro Box

Pyrotechnics

Key

Firing button

CHAPTER 11

PROBLEM-SOLVING

These sections give you not only the solutions to some common problems in theatre but, more importantly, the short cuts. A good starting point is: always label faulty equipment. Otherwise, in the rush to get on with work, it can too easily be recycled back into use, wasting still more time.

LANTERN (LAMP) NOT WORKING

Bulbs are expensive, so check other things before changing one. Has the lantern (lamp) been properly called up on the switchboard? Are there any 'inhibits' in operation, etc.?

Check that the power to the dimmers is switched on. Is the lantern plugged in and in the right socket? Check patching. Try the lantern in a socket that you know is working. Cross-plug it with the one next to it; if it does not work here, the bulb is at fault.

Check the fuse. Remember, the bulb can take out the fuse even after it is blown, so the fuse may need changing more than once, depending on the order in which you try things.

Check the cable. This is a last resort; cable should function properly in a well-maintained theatre.

Check the lantern's internal wiring. If at this stage you are busy, swap lanterns and go back to the dud one later. There is a tendency to overlook the obvious each time one checks, so get someone else to check your thinking.

SMOKING LANTERN

Be ready to fight a fire – but don't get carried away. There is little to burn in a nearly all-metal lantern. Remember too that some gels – browns and chocolates – give off a little vapour when used for the first time, and that gobos made of Lithoplate will also burn off any print still on them. Lanterns should not be rigged touching or close to scenery and drapes.

FUSE KEEPS BLOWING

Check that you are not overloading the circuit. If not, you have a fault somewhere. **Do not try a bigger fuse!** Try to isolate the fault by changing various elements of the rig. The lantern's cable or internal wiring could be shorting out. If in doubt call in an expert.

GOBOS OR GELS BURNING OUT

This happens eventually as part of normal wear and tear, but if it occurs more quickly than is normal the lantern bulb may need realigning. A misaligned bulb can focus too much light and heat on to the gobo or gel. The quickest solution is to focus the lantern differently – lighting design permitting. This is not too difficult with a zoom profile. Home-made gobos can also burn out rather quickly if very fine burring is left on the cut metal. This allows burning to start; so do sharp points in a gobo, particularly in the centre of the lantern's focus. Can the gobo be remade a little differently to avoid this?

LANTERN OUTPUT WEAK

Make sure the switchboard is working properly – that is, the master dimmer has not been knocked down – by comparison with another lantern. Make sure the dimmer is working properly by cross-plugging the lantern with a working circuit. Check the lantern's bulb alignment. This can take time, so if possible swap the lantern and check it later.

SWITCHBOARD NOT WORKING PROPERLY

You should always set a back-up to the lighting if you have the facility. Also make a record of all plotting. Check out whether some part of the board has been used by accident – that is, inhibit switches, blackout faders, etc. Check that all the dimmers and other necessary parts outside the board are receiving power. Some computer-based switchboards react favourably to being switched off and then on gain. Very complex modern boards must not be tampered with without knowledge, but most memory boards are modular and are supplied with replacement parts. Check with the manufacturers, if possible, before attempting even these operations The advantages of memory boards far outweigh the disadvantages caused by failure. If all else fails turn on the working light and call the manufacturer!

CANNOT FIND THE COLOUR YOU WANT

Try another manufacturer's colour range. But you can mix new colours by adding gels together.

NOT ENOUGH LANTERNS

If there are not enough lanterns for a good general cover remember that this is an ideal. Having split the stage into the largest areas that your equipment can cover, you could light each one with a single lantern in front of the stage and slightly off-stage to give some key. See also next points.

THEATRE HAS FEW OR NO BARS TO RIG ON

Check the rigging section for hanging small bars, trapezes, lighting stands and other devices for mounting lanterns. Would the floor space support a number of lighting booms?

TOO FEW LANTERNS TO COVER STAGE OR AREA

Use diffusion to spread available light. Directional diffusion may also be useful.

TOO LITTLE MONEY TO HIRE EQUIPMENT

See the note above. Also, remember when choosing equipment that despite the ideal way of lighting a stage, it can be done less subtly. One or two Fresnels could cover the whole stage, allowing other lanterns to be used as specials.

NOT ENOUGH CIRCUITS

Lanterns can be paired if each socket's dimmer rating allows, though this lessens the rig's flexibility. Parts of the general cover can also be focused to act as specials, in isolation or with other lanterns. Discuss these problems with the director. Perhaps some specials can be re-used where, ideally, different ones would be preferred. Place lanterns where they can be refocused or recoloured during the production. Use follow spots for specials.

TOO LITTLE LIGHT FROM A DARK-COLOURED LANTERN

If you must keep the colour, try piercing the gel to let a little white light mix with the colour, increasing output without changing the colour too much.

PAIRED LANTERNS GIVE DIFFERENT OUTPUTS

Use a colour-correction gel to stop some light output without changing the colour.

TIME RUNNING OUT WHILE RIGGING

Miss out any luxuries in the rig, things you thought of trying but which are not essential. There may be time for them later, though probably not if time is tight at this stage. Check with the production manager whether any more time may be had, explaining your problems. Leave easily accessible rigging – lanterns on stands, floor floods, follow spots – to be done as part of focusing or later. Split the focusing crew to cope with this so that focusing can start.

TIME RUNNING OUT WHILE FOCUSING

Again, leave any 'luxury' lanterns and focus only those which are necessary for plotting. Return to the others later. Also, check scheduling with the production manager. If necessary leave lanterns which are easily explained to the director – for example, a straightforward solo spot as a special in the lighting session – and get back to them later. If more time seems unlikely, try to minimize the work to be done by simplifying the lighting during plotting, but ensuring that it is still effective.

TIME RUNNING OUT WHILE PLOTTING

Plot the cues roughly to get them all in place for the technical rehearsal, or plot only the main lighting moments or blocks. Once a certain number of cues is plotted both you and the director should know where you are heading, and you could finish off the plotting on your own, the director checking the cues and the DSM (first assistant) putting them in the book during the tech. Plotting can continue in the tech though it will make a long session even longer.

NOT GETTING RESULTS DURING PLOTTING

This is difficult. What is presented to the director and designer at this session must not be too much of a surprise. Previous discussions will have covered how the pro-

duction is meant to look. If the director is not happy with what is in the plotting, several roads can be taken:

■ explain your thinking and how you understand it to be what was asked for. The director may then start seeing it in a different and more successful way. Directors must be flexible too!
■ get the director to explain again what is wanted, using the offered lighting as a reference point. Can you then cope by making only minor changes to the rig?
■ offer to change the lighting as the director suggests, but only if you believe what is necessary can be achieved at all with the time and equipment available. It is unfair to offer more than you can deliver.

DARK AREAS ON STAGE

This happens even with the most careful focusing. Lanterns do not always produce equal amounts of light. Some overlap more than others. Isolate offending lanterns and work out what is causing the problem, but be careful. Moving a lantern may only move the dark spot. If you have one it may be easier to rig a new lantern to cover the area, and do some replotting of levels.

ACTORS NOT FINDING THEIR LIGHTS

The actors will want to be where they can be best seen. Talk to them and find out if they really know where they should be, show them where to stand using the light itself. Get them to recognize which light is being used and line themselves up with it. Have a mark put on the stage by the stage management for the actor to find. If all this fails, make the light bigger so that it is easier to get into!

CHAPTER 12

AN INTRODUCTION TO SOUND

Sound effects can make a production, by adding a convincing new texture and reinforcing the setting, atmosphere and mood. The effective use of sound in the theatre is a vital and rewarding part of creating stage pieces – and it is not too difficult to achieve.

SOUND DIRECTION

The lower sound frequencies are better at travelling around and through objects. This is because the slower vibrations are more easily absorbed by the object. For example, a wall can pass on the vibration of a low sound, so we hear the sound through it. The higher frequencies vibrate faster than the wall, so it effectively stops the sound because it is unable to vibrate in unison.

The human brain is good at distinguishing the direction a sound comes from if it is of a high frequency, but not if it is a low one. This is why higher notes are described as directional and lower ones as non-directional.

All these factors must be considered when deciding where to place microphones and loudspeakers.

HOW SOUND IS AMPLIFIED

The vibrations that make up sound can be recorded electrically. Sound vibrations are translated into electrical pulses, and to store sound for later use these pulses have to be permanently recorded on tape or disc.

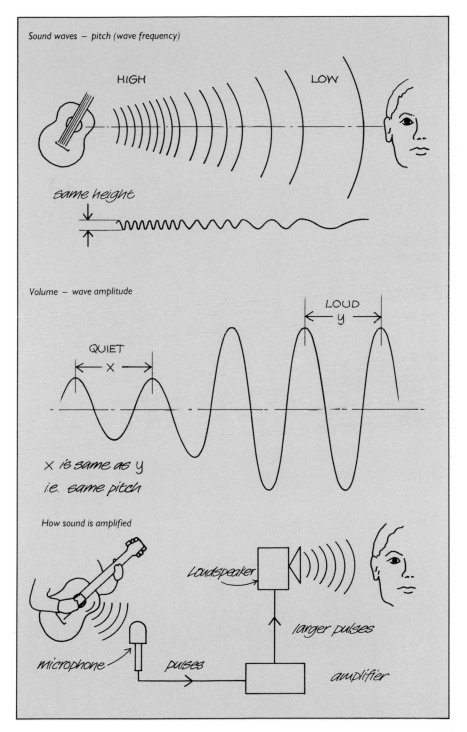

Sound waves — pitch (wave frequency)

HIGH   LOW

same height

Volume — wave amplitude

LOUD
y

QUIET
x

x is same as y
i.e. same pitch

How sound is amplified

Loudspeaker

larger pulses

microphone

pulses

amplifier

79

CHAPTER 13

SOUND RECORDERS

TAPE AND TAPE MACHINES

In theatres sound is most often played from – and recorded on to – a 'reel to reel' tape machine, so called because the tape is stored on reels or spools. The tape recorder uses magnetic tape on which to store sound.

RECORDING ON MAGNETIC TAPE

When sound is recorded on to magnetic tape it is picked up by a microphone and converted into a series of electrical pulses. These are used within a tape machine to generate magnetic fields. The part of the machine that generates these fields is called the recording head. As the tape passes this it takes on the configuration of the magnetic field around it. Thus the sound is recorded on to the tape as a changing series of magnetic messages.

A tape machine has two other heads: *playback* and *erasing*. The former allows pre-recorded tape to be played back.

Note: Care must be taken to keep tapes away from other magnetic sources or they may be ruined. A common source of this disaster is the loudspeaker (see page 92). See also the section below about recording on previously used tape.

TAPE BIAS

In order to get a good recording, tape has to have a certain magnetic reference base. This is known as bias. The tape machine generates bias as it records. It is important that the machine is kept well serviced or this bias will be heard on the tape. For best results the tape machine should be biased for the particular brand of tape used on it. Information about the preferred bias for a tape is usually given by its manufacturer. Biasing of machines is best done by the manufacturers or their agent.

READING THE TAPE-PLAYBACK

To reproduce the sound recorded on to the tape, the machine has a playback head. When the tape passes this head the magnetic message is read from the tape and converted back into electrical pulses, which are then converted into sound.

STEREO RECORDING – TRACKS

On a stereo tape machine the magnetic tape is recorded on in two sections, one for each stereo track. The tracks are referred to as sides of the tape but are actually two halves of the same side. The reverse side of magnetic tape is not usable. Stereo tracks are usually identified as left and right. Multi-track tape machines split the tape up further, but there is a limit to the amount of times the tape can be split before the quality become poor. Tape for tape machines is 5mm (¼in) wide and it is usually not split any more than four ways. Multi-track machines use wider tape for better quality, and more tracks – up to sixty-four.

RECORDING ON USED TAPE AND ERASING

The third head on the tape machine is the erase head. This is used to clear anything recorded on the tape, wiping it clean and making it as new. The three heads on a tape machine are placed so that tape passes them in this order: erase – record – play.

Tape can also be erased using a de-magnetizing device that generates a strong magnetic field to neutralize the changes made to the tape in recording. It is a very fast process as all you have to do is pass the device briefly over the whole spool of tape a few times.

TAPE SPEED AND RECORDING QUALITY

Tape passes through the tape machine at a certain speed. It has to be played back at the speed at which it was recorded. Many machines also have vari-speed which allows small and sensitive adjustments to be made. This is particularly useful for bringing a recorded instrument in tune with one being played live. The faster speeds produce better quality recording. This is because at faster speeds each length of tape has to carry less information.

TAPE MACHINE COMPATIBILITY

Tape machines differ from one manufacturer to another, and even within any given manufacturer's range. If a tape is being made on one machine for use on another, always check that all the following are compatible:

- tape width
- spool size
- speed
- number of tracks

If these factors are all the same then the tape will transfer.

TAPE MACHINE MAINTENANCE

A tape machine must be serviced regularly to keep it in full working order. The theatre technician can help to keep it efficient by following the manufacturer's instructions, particularly by keeping the three heads clean.

CONNECTION TO OTHER MACHINES

The tape deck can be fed a signal (that is, sound as electric pulses) directly from another machine such as a record player. It can

Reel-to-reel tape recorder

also play a signal to other recorders – as well as to an amplifier – to be broadcast. As part of this process the deck can also record live sound via microphones – two for stereo.

Connection of the tape deck to other apparatus, and these to each other, is done with sound cable – care has to be taken to make sure the connectors and the signals produced are compatible (see page 98). This explains why there is more than one type of in-put connector on the tape deck. The many other machines used are dealt with in the next few sections.

CHANNEL SELECTOR

This allows the machine to play back only one of its channels through all of its outputs, to swap over the left track to the right, or record information from the left channel on to the right channel and vice versa.

HEADPHONES

The tape can be listened to using headphones. The headphone level can be changed on the machine. The headphones can monitor either the incoming signal or the tape on the machine.

AUTOMATIC STOP

Most modern tape machines provide for automatic cueing. The automatic stop device stops the tape machine ready for the next cue by recognizing certain points on the tape.

TAPE COUNTER

The tape counter gives a rough indication of whereabouts on the tape you are presently set. All these counters have a certain percentage of inacccuracy, and therefore should not be relied upon to cue or edit tape.

OTHER SOUND RECORDERS AND PLAYERS

Although the tape machine has pride of place in most theatres because it is flexible, reliable and easy to use, other sound recorders and players also play their part. Here is a brief resumé of those instruments and their uses.

CASSETTE TAPE RECORDER

These are used in some theatres mainly because they are cheap. They can be useful in taping and playing back music on pre-recorded cassettes.

As a device to play back sound effects they are difficult to use. Cueing is also very difficult as the tape counter is not accurate enough to set them up precisely for playing and editing. An effect found on cassette would usually be recorded on to a tape machine for ease of editing. Cassette players are used for effects when each one is recorded on to a new cassette and each cassette is carefully cued up before the performance. Even so, the pre-production editing will have to have been done on a tape machine. This use of cassette is only recommended if a tape machine is not available for the performance, as it allows for too many mistakes – choosing the wrong cassette or having a cassette the wrong way round – and is very clumsy.

CARTRIDGE TAPE RECORDER

These machines are much more commonly used in theatres. The tape cartridge consists of a continuous loop of tape. As such they are especially effective for long repetitive sound effects like waves or rain. Because of this, cartridge players have been developed with the sophistication required by the theatre setup, and they can be lined up for accurate cueing.

COMPACT DISC AND RECORD PLAYERS

Music and other effects can be recorded from these disc players. But they are not recommended for use live. It is impossible to find a cue accurately and the needle is too easily knocked out of place (if desperate a cassette player would be preferable). The very sophistication of most compact disc players is a drawback, as timing the finding and playing of any specific track is very difficult. These machines are best left in the sound studio.

CHAPTER 14

MICROPHONES

Although there are many types of microphone they all work in a similar manner. Sound waves vibrate an object, usually a diaphragm, within the microphone. This movement produces the electric pulses that then represent the sound which is carried to amplifier or tape machine.
The microphones most used in theatre work are listed here. The names refer to the way in which the sound waves are converted into electric pulses.

Moving coil
This is both good quality and robust, and therefore the most commonly used theatre microphone. It responds well in the higher frequency range, which includes the human voice.

Condenser
As this is delicate it is only used where it will be reasonablly well cared for, that is, in the sound studio. Its virtue is that it has a flat response to all frequencies and therefore picks up a true reading of any sound.

Ribbon
This is usually sensitive only to sounds in front and behind, not at the sides. Within this range it is extremely sensitive and therefore accurate, but as it is extremely delicate it is seldom used in the theatre.

Experiment with the equipment available to you, preferably in the space in which it will be used. Discover which reproduces the sounds most to your satisfaction. If you encounter difficulties discuss them with the retailer or manufacturer of the equipment, who should be happy to advise you.

MICROPHONE STANDS
Microphones can be supported on stands or attached to clamps. A device can be included as part of these units that prevents any vibrations – causing unnecessary noise – reaching the microphone head. These shock absorbers are especially necessary for microphones attached to the stage floor or scenery. Low floor microphones (floats) are often mounted in foam rubber, when they are called mice – see diagram.

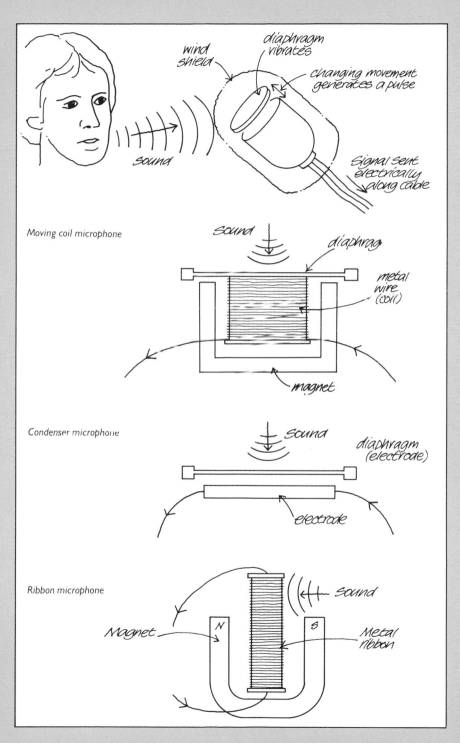

wind
shield

diaphragm
vibrates

changing movement
generates a pulse

sound

Signal sent
electrically
along cable

Moving coil microphone

sound

diaphragm

metal
wire
(coil)

magnet

Condenser microphone

sound

diaphragm
(electrode)

electrode

Ribbon microphone

sound

Magnet

N   S

Metal
ribbon

MICROPHONE DIRECTIONALITY

Microphones differ in the way in which they 'hear' sounds. Some are more sensitive than others to certain areas around them. This is called the directionality of the microphone. Different microphones pick up sounds from one of three different-shaped areas around them. Every different make of microphone will have a different directional character-istic.

Omni-directional microphones

These are especially useful in close-up voice reproduction, as they avoid the problem of the speaker or singer having to speak or sing straight into the mike. As long as they are sufficiently near they will pick up the voice. Small microphones hung around the neck of the performer are omni-directional.

Uni-directional microphones (cardioid)

The area of sensitivy in these is roughly heart-shaped or cardioid, but the actual sha-pe varies greatly from make to make. These are the most useful microphones in theatre use as they only pick up sounds pointed at them, ignoring most unwanted sounds. They are also good for keeping separately-miked sounds apart.

A variation on this shape is the hyper-cardioid microphone which has a pear-shaped catchment area with a rear pick-up.

Bi-directional microphones

The diagram shows why the catchment area of this type is often referred to as a figure eight. Different bi-directional microphones have different figure eights, some being more sensitive at the front than the back. Equally balanced figure eights are particularly useful for recording voices on either side of a microphone. Unequally balanced figure eights are useful for picking up sounds with some added atmospheric sound, such as the voice of a singer with a little of the sound of the audience in the background.

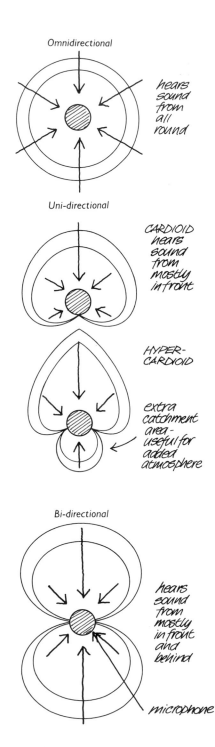

Omnidirectional

hears sound from all round

Uni-directional

CARDIOID hears sound from mostly in front

HYPER-CARDIOID

extra catchment area - useful for added atmosphere

Bi-directional

hears sound from mostly in front and behind

microphone

SPECIALIZED MICROPHONES

There are two types of microphone which have been developed for special purposes.

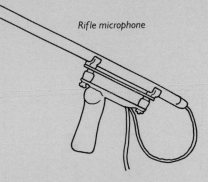

Rifle microphone

Rifle microphones

These are specially adapted to pick up sounds at some distance. They are called rifle or gun microphones as they are long and thin and aimed at the sound. They have an extended front catchment area and will pick up sound at about three times the distance of other microphones.

Radio microphones

These microphones are not connected to the amplifier via a cable, but to a transmitter which broadcasts a radio signal to a receiver. The transmitter can either be part of the microphone or connected to it via a cable. Performers wear these microphones near the mouth, pinned to their clothing, and a fine cable runs underneath to a battery-powered transmitter in a concealed back pocket. The transmitter needs an aerial which can also be easily concealed. The microphone is, of course, omni-directional.

The radio microphone transmits on certain wavelengths. Each microphone in use has a different one, and care must be taken that these are within the band permitted by local authorities. This may result in their picking up other local users such as cab hire firms, but any such problems should become apparent in rehearsal and the frequencies can be changed.

When using radio microphones take care that:

- they are not obstructed by clothing etc.
- the aerials do not get broken or detached
- the batteries are checked and changed regularly
- they are not left on when performers leave the stage. They will not want to be heard offstage!

Radio microphones and receiver

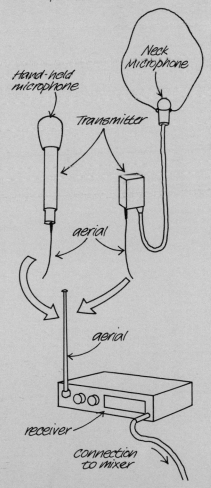

Neck Microphone

Hand-held microphone

Transmitter

aerial

aerial

receiver

connection to mixer

MICROPHONE SET UPS (DIAGRAMS)

When setting up microphones to pick up the sound being made from a musical instrument, including the human voice, certain factors have to be considered:

■ what type of directionality does the microphone we are using have?
■ exactly where does the sound that we are trying to pick up come from?

A large group of musicians can be recorded/amplified as a whole unit by placing several microphones in front of them to pick up the whole sound they produce, as a listener would hear it. For more precise work each instrument will be allocated its own microphone. This allows each individual sound to be balanced against the others, and makes the overall sound even. Certain instruments produce their sound from a large area, and, depending on your resources, more than one microphone may have to be used for a piano or a drum kit.

This can mean having to use a great many microphones. To cut down on the number, a mixture of techniques can be used. First, capture the general sound of the group, and pick out quieter instruments individually. Then, to further decrease the number of microphones used, perhaps it is possible to give instruments like the piano one well-placed microphone.

The piano is an instrument where the source of sounds is spread out, in this case across a large area of strings. To pick up the piano's sounds well, the microphone is not put in a position central to the strings but towards the higher-pitched notes. This is because bass notes travel omni-directionally whereas the higher treble notes are more directional. The bass notes will find the microphone providing it is near enough, whereas the microphone must be pointed towards the treble notes in order for them to be heard well. This is true of all sounds – the lower frequencies being omni-directional, the higher more directional. Thus, if a drum kit has one microphone, it should be put nearer to the cymbal and higher drums than the bass drum.

With singers the omni-directional microphone does not have to be placed directly in front of the mouth. This helps prevent hearing the performer's breathing as well as the voice. If singers do want to sing in to the mike, then certain shields can be put on to prevent this happening. The best technique for using a microphone is to sing or speak over it.

Note: When testing the microphone to see if it is working, do *not* tap it as this can cause great damage. Simply speak into it.

microphones correctly positioned

A microphone has been placed for each part of the drum kit.

PICK-UP.

Microphone placed off-centre near directional treble strings

CHAPTER 15

LOUDSPEAKERS

HOW LOUDSPEAKERS WORK

A loudspeaker works in much the same way as a microphone, but in reverse. In the microphone a diaphragm is moved by sound waves to create an electric pulse; in a speaker the electric pulse vibrates a diaphragm which vibrates the air around it creating sound waves. The diaphragm in a loudspeaker is made in a cone shape.

In order to fill a large auditorium the loudspeaker has to be capable of producing very loud sound over the whole audible range. In order to produce the range the speaker cone has to be able to vibrate at various speeds, to achieve the frequency required. In order to produce the volume the cone has to be able to move backwards and forwards over some distance, to produce the wavelength required. It is very difficult to produce a single loudspeaker that will cope well with all of this, so reproduction of the various ranges is usually done by different speakers within a single loudspeaker cabinet. These loudspeakers are popularly known as woofers and tweeters.

WOOFERS AND TWEETERS

The low frequencies are produced by larger loudspeakers: the woofers. They produce the correct low frequency by vibrating a large amount of air slowly.

The higher frequencies are reproduced by smaller loudspeakers: the tweeters. They produce the correct high frequency by vibrating a small amount of air very quickly. The cone of most loudspeakers is usually made of stiff but flexible paper. But at very high frequencies the movement is so fast that paper would not last long, so some tweeters have thin metal cones, usually disc shaped. In this case the speaker is called a horn.

The tweeter and the woofer overlap slightly in order to reproduce the whole of the necessary sound. But to cope with the frequencies in the middle of the range a third speaker is often included.

CROSSOVER

A tweeter would be damaged if it received the electric pulses meant for the woofer, and vice versa. So a device is included to send the correct part of the signal to the correct device. This is the crossover.

LOUDSPEAKER CONNECTIONS

Loudspeakers are connected to the amplifier via two lines, positive and negative. If you are only using one speaker it does not matter which connects to which. But with two or more speakers it is important that they are all connected the same way so that they are in phase. Otherwise when the speaker cones vibrate, one speaker's cone will be going in when the other's is going out. This causes a loss of quality (particularly in the bass frequencies), and of volume. (See also the section on connecting all the equipment, page 98.)

VOLUME

Speaker power is measured in watts. On average, domestic loudspeakers are 30 watts. A large auditorium would require several loudspeakers of up to 100 watts. The wattage is not necessarily always an indication of loudness. The manufacturers can be consulted or as mentioned before, a comparative experiment made. Remember that the loudspeaker must not be over-loaded by the amplifier. To prevent damage they often have their own fuses.

SPEAKER RANGE

A good loudspeaker will project sound over a range of 40°-60° horizontally, and 20°-30° vertically. Manufacturers will provide information concerning individual models.

CHOOSING LOUDSPEAKERS AND CABINETS

The cabinets in which the loudspeakers sit are also important. They can help aim the sound in the same direction as the speaker is pointing. There are several designs manufactured. As with speakers, on different cabinets the same sound signal can appear to have more bass, treble or middle range. Sound designers always have their particular favourites. The best way of deciding, if you have a choice, is to ask for a demonstration. Better still, ask to try various speakers and compare them in the space where you will be working. Bear in mind that the surroundings also affect the quality of sound. When the set is in place it may seem different.

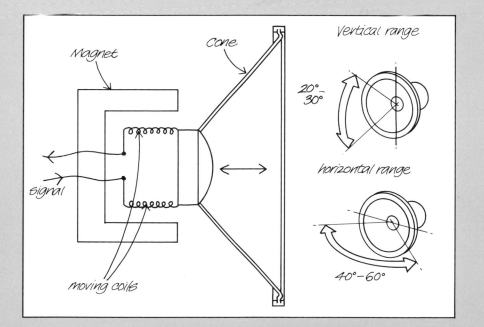

Magnet

Cone

signal

moving coils

Vertical range

20°-30°

horizontal range

40°-60°

POSITIONING LOUDSPEAKERS

Before hanging any loudspeakers make sure that they are properly secured.

INITIAL FACTORS

The way loudspeakers are placed affects the way in which the sound is heard. It is difficult for an audience to distinguish direction – left and right – if the angle between the speakers is small. Therefore, loudspeakers that are upstage need not be as precisely placed as those that are downstage, nearer the audience. If the sound is supposed to be coming from a prop, such as a radio, the speaker should be placed near to it, ideally inside it. If this is impossible place the speaker in a direct line between the audience and the prop.

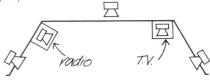

Sound will not travel through certain materials. If the speaker has to be hidden behind an object it is best if the object is made of a thin material. Cloth with a weave opening of 50 per cent or more will not interfere with the sound at all. Gauze or speaker cabinet material is ideal. If the speaker has to be placed behind something more solid, either drill small holes to let the sound through, or move the speaker back to allow some of the sound to get round it. Take care not to leave objects on, or directly in front of, the speakers during the performance.

ACOUSTICS

The factors affecting how sound moves around a certain space are varied, extremely complex, and mostly the concern of architects. But ensuring that performers can be clearly heard in any auditorium involves understanding a few relatively simple rules. These rules will further affect the positioning of speakers.

To begin we must consider further how the brain analyses sound.

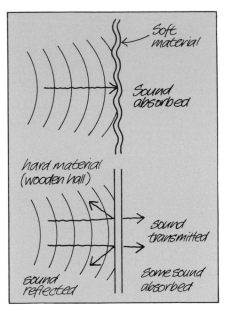

HEARING SOUND

The brain receives information about sound from two instruments: our ears. It analyses this information, and thus we hear in stereo. The brain can be fooled by the clever positioning of loudspeakers, and the use of amplified sound, into believing that it is hearing things that it is not. The diagram shown here demonstrates how this can be done.

STEREO SPEAKER POSITIONS

On hearing equally balanced sound coming from a pair of speakers positioned one to the left, and one to the right, the human brain will believe that the sound comes from a point between them. So if the two speakers in our sound design on either side of the performer are used at equal volumes, a listener sitting equidistant between the two will believe that the sound is coming from the performer.

In order to alter where the sound seems to be coming from, the volumes can be changed accordingly. More volume from the speaker on the left will appear to move the sound in that direction. This will only work in some auditorium shapes – if the audience is spread across the width of the stage they cannot all be catered for using this system. But if there is sufficient distance from the stage to the front row, large numbers of the audience can be fooled. Alternatively, speakers can be placed above the stage.

SPEAKERS ABOVE THE STAGE

Because our ears are on either side of our heads the brain is good at analysing sound on the horizontal axis but not the vertical.

If in our sound design a loudspeaker to the far left is used, the sound will be detected as coming from there, giving the audience the impression that the performer is throwing her voice. But if the speaker is placed far above the performer the problem does not occur. Our brains are not able to distinguish between the position of the speaker and the position of the performer.

So if the speakers cannot be built in to the set, or a stereo pair of speakers used, a good speaker position is above the stage.

SPEAKER POSITIONS IN A LARGE AUDITORIUM

In a theatre of considerable size, or on more than one level, speakers may have to be placed forward of the stage to reach the far seating positions. Turning up the volume does not solve the problem as this would also result in members of the audience closer to the stage finding the sound level uncomfortably loud. Speakers placed closer to the distant audience follow the same rules as those described above: i.e. overhead positions are preferable. This is not always

possible, but another phenomenon concerning how the brain hears sounds can come to the rescue: sound delay.

SOUND DELAY

The human brain is used to coping with natural echo. It will believe that of two identical sounds, the one it hears first represents the true direction of the source of that sound. This can have an adverse effect where speakers are placed to provide sound for people at some distance from the stage. Because these speakers are closer the sound coming from them will reach the audience *before* sound coming from the onstage speakers. The brain will believe that the true direction of this sound is from these nearer speakers. This could be disastrous, particularly if these speakers have had to be placed to the side of the audience. Those at the back will see someone singing in front of them but hear them from the side!

The solution is to delay the sound from the nearer speakers so that it arrives at the audience a fraction of a second behind the sound coming from the stage speakers. Even if the volume of sound from the nearer speakers is much greater, the brain will still believe all the sound is coming from the stage! This is done by installing a sound delay system.

DIRECTING THE AMPLIFIED VOICE AND FEEDBACK

When working out the direction in which to point speakers always remember that it is the higher frequencies over which we have most control, the bass frequencies being non-directional. Fortunately the human voice is in the higher part of the range.

Also consider the possibilty of feedback. This is caused by the amplified sound being fed back into the microphones that are picking up the original sound. It is possible to avoid problems by directing the speakers out to the audience from in front of the microphone positions. But if no microphones are in use for sound effects this is not a problem.

CHAPTER 16

SOUND MIXERS AND AMPLIFIERS

The sound mixer does just that. It takes the signals that represent sound from various devices and allows them to be mixed. It will accept and mix signals from record decks, cassette decks, tape decks and microphones. The number of signals that a mixer will receive is dictated by the particular model in use. The diagram shows a typical one.

CHANNELS AND CHANNEL FADERS

The signals enter the mixer and are allocated to a different channel on the mixer. These are numbered for easy identification. To hear all the tracks on a four-track tape deck, four channels are used. A stereo signal uses two channels. The channels are graduated so that each can be set to a different level and faded up and down. The graduations are usually in points (one to ten) or decibels, the measurement of sound intensity or volume. The level set on a channel dictates the level at which the signal will be sent out of the mixer to the amplifier and then the loudspeaker. Adjusting the channels to different levels allows the different sounds to be played back at different relative volumes, thus achieving a good sound balance.

Each channel also has a number of other controls that allow the sound signal to be altered:

■ the type of signal to be used can be selected, that is, at mike or line intensity
■ the volume of the incoming signal can be set using a *gain control*
■ the signal can be allocated to various output channels, and through them to amplifiers and loudspeakers
■ the signal can be faded from one set of output channels to another *(panning)*
■ the tone of the signal can be adjusted – various degrees of treble or bass added or subtracted
■ echoes can be added.

The mixer will also have *level indicators* on each channel showing the level of the signal being generated from it. This can be a LED display but is more usually a meter. *Peak indicators* show when the volume of signal being used reaches a point where the machine can no longer prevent distortion. The peak control is often a feature of the level meter.

MASTER FADERS

As seen above the volume and quality of an incoming signal are set at the channel, and allocated one or more outputs. The output channels are also governed by controls: a fader for each one. These are called the master faders. Each output is usually connected to a single amplifier, and often each amplifier will drive only one loudspeaker.

Thus, these controls relate directly to the speakers in use. Again the faders are numbered and graduated, usually from one to ten.

These controls also have some of the features of the input channels, allowing further changes to be made to the sound. Tone controls, echo and prefade are usual.

DESCRIBING THE MIXER

Mixers are described by the number of input and output channels. A mixer with eight inputs and two outputs would be described as an "eight into two".

Mixers often have many additional features as described on the next page.

Sound mixer

MIXER FACILITIES

Different models of mixer will have different additional facilities, but the following are to be expected.

Headphone socket

This allows the operator to listen to the sound mix. If the sound is being used as only part of a scene it is sometimes difficult for the operator to hear clearly whether the sound mix is correct.

Prefade listen

This allows the operator to listen on headphones to the sound signal as it enters the channel, before being affected by the mixer, and thus assess its quality.

Sub-grouping

The sub-groups allow a mixed sound signal to be further adjusted before finally leaving the mixer through the output channels. Therefore the sub-groups can be seen as divisions of the output channels, allowing various groups of mixed sound to be differently adjusted.

The sub-groups will therefore have tone, pan, prefade and other such controls.

Foldback

A special type of sub-group allows for foldback. This is the ability to send the mixed sound signal to certain speakers which are placed to allow the people making the sound to hear themselves.

Auxiliary outputs

The mixer also provides extra output channels so that further external devices can be used to change the quality of the sound. These can include echo machines and delay machines. For example, the sound coming from the input channels can be sent via the auxiliary output to a delay machine, delayed, then sent back into another mixer channel to be sent out to the correct amplifier and

loudspeaker. The fully mixed signal could also be treated in this manner. (See other sound equipment, page 97.)

MIXER OPERATION

See sound operating procedures, page 109.

AMPLIFIERS

Until it reaches the amplifier the sound signal is quite small. It is the amplifier that increases the strength of the signal in order that it can drive a loudspeaker at volume. It is important to use a good amplifier so that in increasing the sound signal no distortion occurs. The speaker must be properly matched to the loudspeakers it is asked to drive. Too great an output from the amplifier will damage the speaker and too little will require the speaker to be driven at a very high level which may cause it to distort the sound signal.

The most flexible system allows each amplifier to be allocated to one speaker only. Because of this it is common for amplifiers to be built in units of two or four.

Controls

The amplifier is quite a simple piece of equipment. It will have a power switch, level control and indicator. The level control allows the amplifier itself to dictate the level of output it is generating. Amplifiers with more controls are really mixer amplifiers.

MIXER/AMPLIFIERS

The mixer/amplifier is a combination of both machines. Usually the mixer part will not be as sophisticated as the mixer previously described. It may just have a few tone controls (treble and bass), a gain control, and mike/line allocation. Mixer/ampifiers are particularly popular for public address systems, and useful in rehearsals, but usually do not have the sophistication or power to be of use in the theatre context.

CHAPTER 17

OTHER SOUND EQUIPMENT

The sound system is made up of a source machine, tape deck or microphone, a mixer, amplifiers and loudspeakers. Although this may be sufficient for most purposes there are other machines that can be connected into the system to further control the quality and character of the sound.

GRAPHIC EQUALIZERS

The graphic equalizer is a sophisticated tone control which divides up the sound signal into various frequencies. It allows the volume of each band of frequencies to be raised or lowered. It usually deals with the whole sound signal after it has left the mixer or before it reaches each group of loudspeakers.

This machine is especially useful in changing sound to suit a particular building or space, the sound operator leaving it set for the theatre space rather than using it for subtle alterations of individual sound cues.

Graphic equalizers can be set for maximum effect using your own ears or a device called a spectrum analyser.

SPECTRUM ANALYSER

This gives an accurate display of how a sound is affected by the space in which it is played. For example, a known sound is played into the room. The spectrum analyser will display which frequencies are en-

hanced by the space and which are dulled. The graphic equaliser can then be set to increase the dulled bands and decrease the enhanced bands. This process can continue until the frequency response of the room is generally even.

ECHO MACHINE

This is used to increase the reverberation of a sound. This can have the effect of enhancing its quality, or of producing a noticeable echo when required.

SOUND DELAY MACHINE

The sound delay machine is used to delay the sound to one set of speakers against another.

NOISE GATE

This device only allows sound of a certain volume to be fed into the mixer. The noise gate can be set to relay only the sound of the instrumentalist and to cut out completely when the sound level drops to background noise.

SAMPLER

This device will sample a sound – live or recorded – to which sophisticated and sensitive adjustments can then be made, for example a singer singing out of tune could be tuned correctly; or a church bell chime could have its pitch changed to produce a chimneypiece clock chiming.

CHAPTER 18

THE WHOLE SOUND SYSTEM

A sound system is constructed by connecting together the equipment described in the previous chapters.
This chapter describes all the connectors and cable required to connect the sound system together.

CONNECTING EQUIPMENT

To find out whether the equipment in use is compatible and can be successfully connected you must check the following details: signal level, impedance and balance.

SIGNAL LEVEL

The signal level between all the equipment *before reaching the amplifier* is very low, usually no higher than 3 volts. The signal levels are measured in volts or decibels, for example 3 volts equals 6.6 decibels. The range is divided into two categories: microphone level and line level. Microphone levels are very small (-80 dB to -20 dB). Line levels (as from tape decks) are higher (-20 dB to 0 dB). Sound mixers will usually have both mike and line level inputs, switchable on the main console. Microphones are also operated on two levels of *impedance*.

IMPEDANCE

This is a form of electrical resistance found in a/c circuits. Like resistance it is measured in ohms.

Impedance and microphones

Because the signal level is so low in microphones the impedance can be a large factor in the quality of the sound produced. Depending on the manner in which it converts the sound to an electrical signal, the microphone can have high or low impedance. The commonly used theatre microphones are low impedance (30-600 ohms). These include the ribbon microphone (30-50 ohms) and the condenser and moving coil microphones (200-300 ohms).

Note: A low-impedance microphone may produce satisfactory results in a high-impedance input, but with lack of volume. The reverse will not work: bad distortion of the sound will occur.

Impedance and loudspeakers

The impedance of a loudspeaker varies from between 2-30 ohms. Amplifiers must be used that can cope with the impedance of the speaker. If the speaker has an impedance lower than the amplifier, the sound may be distorted and the amplifier damaged. If the speaker has a higher impedance than the amplifier, the sound level will be low.

BALANCE

An unbalanced line is one that uses a single wire for the sound signal and an earth. Because the sound signals are so weak interference can be a problem. A balanced line is one that has an earth and two signal lines running out of phase. Any interference affects both lines but as they are out of phase the interference is cancelled out. To prevent interference balanced cables are used in theatres, whereas most domestic sound systems with short cables use simpler and cheaper unbalanced cables.

There are also other kinds of interference.

SOUND INTERFERENCE

The relative weakness of the electrical signal used in sound systems can cause problems with interference, even in the stronger speaker signal.

Unbalanced sound cables receive interference from the electro-magnetic fields generated by nearby electric equipment and cables. This kind of interference usually adds a hum to the sound. To solve this the cable should be kept well away from such dangers. But the use of a balanced line as described above is a better solution.

Interference can also be caused from the current generated in the earth – this being by definition connected to all the other equipment in the system. In an unbalanced line system, interference of this kind is best solved by disconnecting the earths from all but one of the pieces of equipment in use. **This can be dangerous,** and should only be tried on equipment that forms a permanent stationary system. In a balanced system, earth interference is solved by disconnecting one end of the earth line of the cable.

Interference can also be caused by electrostatic fields, like radio signals. Here the cable, or more likely the earth network, is acting as a large aerial. This is solved by surrounding the cable with a braided metalic shield or screen. This is usually also the earth line.

A a general rule, to prevent interference cables should not run besides normal power leads, or near other electrical equipment, electric switches or power supplies. If the sound cable has to cross a power cable make sure it crosses at 90° thereby making as little contact as possible.

Note: One of the worst offenders regarding sound interference is the lighting dimmer, so keep the sound cables well away.

CABLE CONNECTORS

There are many kinds of connector. Here are the most commonly used:

Phono connector
Robust: Yes
Uses: Non-stage equipment: record, cassette and tape decks
Type: ??

Mini jackplug
Robust: No
Uses: Domestic
Types: Mono and stereo

DIN connectors
Robust: No
Uses: Domestic only
Types: Three, four, five pin

Jackplug
Robust: Yes, especially metal clad
Uses: Loudspeakers and microphones
Type: Mono and stereo

Cannon or LXR
Robust: Yes, can also be locked in place
Uses: Loudspeakers and microphones
Type: Three pin (microphone) and four pin (loudspeaker); male and female

PATCHING SYSTEMS

Many permanent sound installations use patching systems to avoid the need for rigging and de-rigging long cable runs for each production. Patching systems work by having permanent cable runs for microphones and loudspeakers, terminating in groups of sockets. Several groups will be found around the stage, and the other end of the run will be terminated in the sound control area. The robust XLR connector will be used in such an installation.

MAKING A RECORDING

CHAPTER 19

THE SOUND STUDIO

The illustration opposite shows how sound equipment is best arranged to maximize efficiency when making a sound tape. The sound studio should ideally be soundproof to prevent any extraneous noises being recorded when using microphones. A good studio will have a separate room for live recording, visible through soundproof glass. Such a layout keeps the noises of the equipment and the people working it away from the microphones.

Light signals, or a talkback system, are essential for communicating with the recording room.

Ideally the sound studio will have an index of sound effects already available on records and tapes.

RECORDING METHODS

The first step to getting good recordings is to use the best equipment, regularly cleaned and serviced. To protect the mechanisms always start the recording with the channels down: do not guess a level. Too big a signal can ruin the equipment.

Next, *take your time.* The work done in the studio will dictate the effectiveness of the sound in the theatre. There may not be time later for delicate adjustments.

Last, *be well organized,* especially if your time in the studio is limited. Work out beforehand what you have to do and make a list.

SOUND LEVELS

When recording on to tape it is important to get a good loud recording with no extraneous sounds. Make sure you are using the correct input on the tape deck. Use the level meters on the tape machine to get a good level. The meters will display the sound level and show when it is distorting. The recording should be as close to the upper limit as possible.

A good sound level on the recording will reduce the need for too much amplification later. If it is too quiet the amplification level in the theatre may have to be high, causing any background hiss on the recording to become audible as well. Too high a recorded level will cause distortion on the tape itself, which cannot be cured later.

Experiment with different parts of the sound to be recorded before setting the final recording level, as it may vary a great deal in intensity. This also applies if the sound is being created live. A dummy run should discover how the performers are going to use the microphones and what the levels will be. If necessary advise them how to make best use of the mikes.

Recordings with a large variation of sound levels, which produce only momentary highs, briefly evident as distortion on the tape deck, may sound acceptable. But when you get to know the way the sound works, a little cheating with levels during the recording session can help matters. Remember that the tape deck will let you monitor the incoming signal as well as the recording being made.

Monitor speaker

Tape machine

Cassette player

Record deck

Effects on compact disc

Mixer

MIXING SOUND ON TO TAPE

Working without a mixer

Some sound tapes will not need a mixer in their making, and only one tape deck. For example, a straightforward piece of music can be recorded directly on to the tape.

Sometimes a mixer is simply not available, but you can still create sound tapes of some complexity. Sound cannot be overlaid on a single track of tape: the tape recorder erases each track just before it is re-recorded over. But as most tape decks are at least two-track machines, it is possible to put different sounds on the two tracks. Playing these tracks back in mono will produce a mixed sound effect, for example wind and rain. Reverberation and echo effects can also be added without the aid of such devices on a sound mixer.

When using a tape deck in this way, make sure the whole of the source signal is switched to the single track being used. On most tape decks the tracks are selected by switching off the recording device on the track not being used. Remember to check that you have switched tracks before recording the second one.

Working with a mixer

Using a sound mixer in the sound studio opens up many more possibilities. Many different sound signals can be played into the tape recorder. This results in a rather complicated number of devices and actions taking place at once. For example, on a two-track machine: track one records, from two record decks, sea lapping and gulls crying; track two records performers making the noises of people rowing a boat over several microphones.

The alternative to this rather complex arrangement is the use of more than one tape deck, in which case the studio mixer can be a smaller and simpler one than that used in the theatre.

USING TWO TAPE DECKS

The provision of more than one tape deck in a sound studio allows for tape-to-tape recording, and makes it possible to build a sound tape out of any number of effects.

For example, using two-track machines a recording is made using both tracks on machine one. These are then both played on to one track only of machine two. A new recording is made using both tracks of machine one and these are re-recorded on to the second track of machine two. The sound tape on machine two now has four different sound effects on it.

This process can go on for ever, the tape on machine two being played back on to only one track on machine one, leaving a track for another similarly produced sound effect, and bringing the number of tracks to eight, and so on.

Each time a recording is made some loss of quality results. But by using a simple mixer and two tape decks the amount of re-recording can be kept to a minimum.

Over-complication

Do not get carried away: a finished sound tape can be *too* complicated. Rather than mix together many different tracks of sea, wave, wind and gulls for a sound effect it may be better to keep things simple. The director may want to balance the sound level of the gulls against that of the sea, which can only be done if they are on separate tracks.

CHANGING THE QUALITY OF THE RECORDING

The quality of the original sound can be changed before it is recorded as well as after. But a heavily altered recorded track cannot be restored by the playback devices. For example, added treble on the recording can be subdued by using the mixer when it is played back to subtract the treble frequencies, but the original neutral balanced sound will not be restored. So take care when making the recording not to produce something that will prove inflexible in the theatre. You must use your judgement as to whether changing the quality of a recording will enhance it or make it less useful.

Simple experimentation will soon show you how you can obtain the recording effects required by changing tone, speed or pitch, or by creating an echo (see also cartridge tape recorders, page 82).

CHAPTER 20
EDITING AND SPLICING

City of Westminster College
Paddington Learning Centre
25 Paddington Green
London W2 1NB

JOINING TOGETHER SOUND EFFECTS

Pieces of magnetic tape can be joined together or cut up to create a single sound effect. Similarly a series of sound effects can be joined together to make a complete sound tape. The process is called editing; the method is called splicing. Splicing tape is very easy and, with practice, can be carried out very quickly. But take care not to introduce twists in the tape.

TYPES OF EDIT

Different sound effects will require different types of editing when the sounds are joined together. This is why the editing block has more than one angle on it at which to cut the tape. The obvious cut is 90°, straight-cross. This brings one effect right up against another and may produce a discernible click. So angled cuts – 60° and 45° – are used to prevent this. This way the whole of the join does not pass in front of the playback head all at once. The 45° angle can be difficult to join precisely as it makes for very thin wedges of tape so generally the 60° angle is used.

Experience will soon show you when to use the different edits. For example:

■ two explosions, one interrupting the other: 90° edit
■ a piece of music stopping and then another following on: 60° edit
■ one wind sound effect joining another with a change of pitch: 45° edit.

FINISHED SOUND TAPE

A full sound tape does not just consist of one sound effect joined to the next and so on. To make the cueing easier and more reliable, each sound sequence is separated by a special piece of tape which identifies it. This is called leader tape because it leads into the sound cue.

LEADER TAPE

Leader tape is spliced into the sound tape in exactly the same way as described above for editing different sounds together. It comes in many colours and in white. There are two preferred methods for using leader tape to make each sound cue easily identifiable. Which you find best will be partly personal preference, partly the particular circumstances.

Method one
Each sound cue can be allocated its own colour leader tape. The colour of each cue should be noted on the sound operator's

cue sheet (see page 120). Take care that in the operating situation no two colours can be confused.

Method Two

Alternatively use white leader tape only and record information about each cue on it in ink. Problems with this method arise if the operating situation is too dim to read by, or if the tape machine position makes it difficult to see the leader.

EDITING EFFECTS

The joining together of sound effects allows many sounds to follow each other without the need for complicated mixing or equipment. The technique of editing needs only a minimum of equipment and space and can therefore be performed wherever the tape deck is placed. This means that basic editing can be done in the theatre quite quickly. A small editing kit (blade, editing block and reel of tape) should always be on hand for emergencies.

Editing tape together also allows for the use of automatic cueing devices and a quick solution to the making of very long repetitive sound cues.

AUTOMATIC STOPS

Most modern tape machines have a device (usually optical) which will identify certain types of tape, and on doing so stop the tape machine. The special tapes can be edited into the sound effects tape, as part of the leader, so that the tape will automatically

stop in the correct place for the next sound cue to be played.

SOUND LOOPS

The recording of long sound effects from small sound sources can be very tedious. These sound effects can be cut together, but producing a 20-minute sound effect of lapping waves from a 20-second sound effects track would be very tedious and involve over 60 separate recordings, not to mention the edits! The problem is solved by making a sound loop.

This involves recording the sound effect once and then carefully editing the two ends of the tape together. Often this has to be attempted several times before a satisfactory edit is achieved; it has to be perfect because it will be heard many times on the finished sound cue.

The loop is made by threading the tape through the machine heads and out into the sound studio, where it has to be supported so that the weight of the tape does not drag on the rest of the tape too much. The tape is then taken over the pick-up spool and across to the original spool where the join is made. The length of the tape dictates the length of its journey around the studio. The tape machine will pull the tape along provided it is not allowed to drag too much.

The tape is played, and the resultant sound recorded on to an ordinary reel of tape on another machine. The loop can go on being recorded for as long as is necessary.

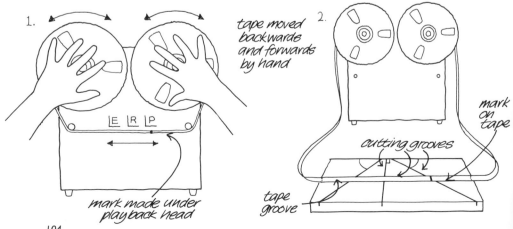

1. tape moved backwards and forwards by hand

E R P

mark made under playback head

2. mark on tape

cutting grooves

tape groove

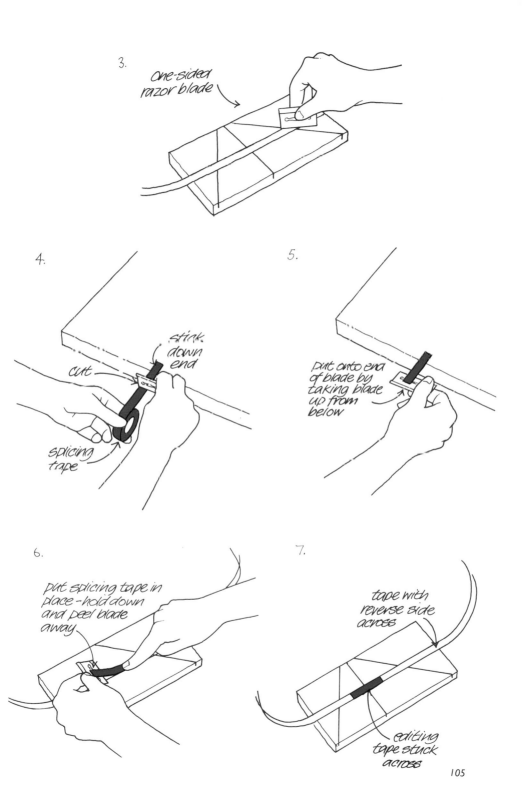

3.

One-sided razor blade

4.

cut

stick down end

splicing tape

5.

put onto end of blade by taking blade up from below

6.

put splicing tape in place – hold down and peel blade away

7.

tape with reverse side across

editing tape stuck across

105

MAKING A SOUND EFFECTS TAPE

CHAPTER 21

NOTE TAKING

It is essential to take clear notes during the process of making a sound effects tape. Magnetic tape does not change in appearance when it has been used, neither does it show what has been recorded on it. Because of this, clear notes and annotation of the tapes in use must be made. Making an effects tape of any length involves days of work, and before the final editing the recorded sounds are kept on many different spools. All of these, if not properly labelled, can only too easily be mislaid, or worse, recorded over.

THE TEXT AND THE DIRECTOR

Making a sound effects tape for a particular production calls for a number of things, but, as always, the text is the natural starting point: read it carefully. The sound designer is looking for two things: the author's descriptions of the settings that detail sounds or suggest them, and moments in the piece that suggest sound effects. The director will approach the text in a similar way, and the two of you should work together from an early stage.

Some directors will also want to surround the production with music, possibly before,

after and during each scene. Some directors will even go as far as requiring a film-type sound track backing all the action. There is rarely the money to have such music composed and recorded especially for the production, so directors must rely on their own ideas and those of the sound designer. A wide knowledge of recorded music is helpful.

It is important to understand the director's ideas fully. If you are unsure make a point of playing the director any work you have done as soon as it is recorded and mixed. He or she can then make comments and suggest how it can be changed to fit more exactly with what they had in mind. Be prepared to make helpful suggestions, including using more or less sound than the director may initially be thinking of. If a sound effect is to be thrown out because it is wrong, it is best to do this early rather than late.

Remember that some sound effects may sound better performed just offstage (see live sound effects, page 112).

STARTING WORK: PRODUCTION MEETING

The sound designer should start by making a list of the cues required in the order that they will be used. If cues overlap they may have to be mixed together on tape. If these cues all have to be brought into the action of the play at precise moments, more than one tape deck may have to be used. If the initial sound list seems to require more pieces of equipment than are actually available, go to the production manager to request money from the show budget to hire or buy more, or to the director to suggest how compromises could be made. The production meeting is a good place to raise these problems.

This meeting is also another opportunity to find out more about how the director wants to use sound as part of the production, and how sound fits into its whole shape. It is important not to work in isolation, and to make the production work as a whole rather than many separate parts.

SOUND MEETINGS

Having decided on the number and order of sound cues required for a production the sound designer must do some research. Sources of the sound effects and music have to be found.

The sound designer may have strong ideas as to what the effects should sound like, but it is best to find as many options as are available for the sound cues required and then call an initial sound meeting with the director. At this meeting play the director the options for each sound cue so that he or she can make a choice. On hearing the options the director may suggest mixing some of the sounds together, trying a totally different idea for the effect, cutting the sound cue altogether, or looking for better source material.

In any case there will probably be enough problems to result in several more sound meetings being necessary.

RECORDING

As part of the process of making the sound tape, recordings may have to be made involving certain performers. When this is the case make sure a copy is made of the initial recording before editing occurs. While an effect can be re-recorded from a record as many times as may be necessary, it will be a waste of other people's time to organize another recording session. Indeed it may not be possible to re-create such effects again!

REHEARSALS

The sound designer should also keep in touch with rehearsals, either through the stage management team or directly. A good team will issue rehearsal reports, and these must be checked for any relevant information. It is a good idea to try and attend the rehearsal of any parts of the play that require complicated sound sequences, if not all the play. You may need to see how a scene is played in order to be able to edit the cues on to the sound tape(s) in the correct order. Also you may be able to suggest better ways of using sound after seeing a rehearsal.

It is essential to get a good timing of the length of the sound cues, and this can only really be achieved accurately in rehearsals. It can be very frustrating to make a sound cue only to find during the technical rehearsal that it is not long enough

Note: It is better to make too much tape than to try and be precise. Timings change, and it is far easier to edit tape out than stretch a cue!

Rehearsal tape

It is a good idea to make a rough tape to be used in rehearsals so that the actors, stage management, and director all get used to working with the sound cues. Directors will often ask for one. Prepare a rough version of the important cues, without clever mixing etc., and put them on to cassette tapes. In rehearsals the stage manager can then select the tape containing the relevant cue and play it on a portable tape machine. The finished sound cues could also be put into rehearsals in this way, only in this case on a single tape, but without the gaps caused by leader tape.

FINISHING THE TAPE

The final part of making an effects tape involves joining all the recordings that are going to be used in order, with leader tape and, if applicable, automatic stops. When this is done it is a good idea to copy all the sound effects on to a spare tape without leaders. Accidents can happen, and it is as well to be able to replace any cue immediately.

CHAPTER 22

WORKING IN THE THEATRE

RIGGING AND TESTING

The sound team will be allocated time to put the relevant sound equipment into the theatre space. Speakers and microphones may have to be hung above the stage or auditorium, and as with the lanterns they must be safely chained in place. Speakers and microphones may also have to be built into the set. The tape machines, mixers and other equipment will all have to be placed in their operating positions.

THE OPERATING POSITION

As with stage lighting control, the time when the operator lurked in the wings is over. The sophisticated use to which sound is now put requires a good operating position, somewhere out with the audience. It is important to operate sound from a position where the operator has a chance to hear the effects properly. A clear view of the stage is also an advantage.

Too often sound operators share the operating position of the lighting control equipment; this is usually not good enough and should be resisted. Theatre lighting control boxes are usually enclosed environments where the sound of the action on stage is relayed over the theatre's intercom system. This is of no use to the sound operator. It is impossible to operate sound with sensitivity from a position where what is heard depends on a mere sound relay system.

Ideally the operating position should be such that the operator is in the audience. Directly behind the last row of seats is usually a good position.

Lighting control boxes are also notoriously placed so that while the operator has a clear view of the stage it is from a rather strange angle. Again it is important for the sound operator to be seated fairly centrally, so that a good sound balance can be achieved. This becomes imperative for the mixing of live sound.

PLOTTING THE SOUND

The sound effects have to be plotted into the production. The deputy stage manager has to put the cues in the book (the master copy of the script) and the operator must be told what is required. It is best to have a specific time allocated on the production schedule for this. If there are only a few sound cues it is possible, although not desirable, to plot the sound during the technical rehearsal.

Plotting recorded effects

This involves playing each sound cue and setting the level at which it should be played as well as any other necessary information such as tone alterations, loudspeaker selection, panning information etc. If microphones are involved their use should also be treated as a cue. The sound operator should write down all the information required to operate each sequence of cues.

Plotting live sound

If there is a lot of live sound and live mixing involved in a production then a separate music plotting session should be incorporated as part of the production schedule. This session should never be incorporated in to the technical rehearsal, but should take place before the production week, specifically to ensure that the technical rehearsal is a smoother and shorter affair. (See mixing live sound, Page 110.)

THE SOUND PLOT

Sound-plotting sheets vary depending on the equipment in use, specifically the mixer. They should have positions to mark all the information required to operate the sound effects accurately. There can be many individual operations involved with each cue – tone controls, panning, channel levels, master fader levels, tape deck, input switching etc. Because of this the plotting sheets should be kept as simple as possible. (See the example.)

Apart from the plotting session described above, and the obvious following of the sound plot, there are other facets to operating sound. It is particularly important that the sound operator does not work as an automaton. No two performances are the same and some artistic judgement is required on even the simplest sound effects. This often involves the volume of the effect. The size of the audience will affect the acoustics of the auditorium, and different audiences will make different amounts of noise during a performance, especially in a comedy where they will laugh in entirely different places from night to night. Also performers will use differing techniques and possibly alter their positions in relation to microphones.

In all these cases the sound operator, along with the DSM who is running the show, has to make a decision on altering the sound levels to compensate for this. Sensitivity is called for. (See also problems solved, page 118.)

Note: A sound effect cue is often abbreviated to 'FX cue'. Take care not to cause confusion in the cueing procedure with the abbreviation for a lighting cue of 'LX cue'. 'Sound cue' may be a better option.

MIXING LIVE SOUND

The mixing of recorded sound can be extremely difficult, the mixing of live sound even more so. With live sound the factors that can effect the quality of the sound being amplified are multiplied, and vary from moment to moment. Live mixing involves a variety of techniques.

Rehearsing

Unlike a recorded effect, the sound is likely to change greatly, due to the performer's mood from performance to performance. It is therefore worth putting the equipment that is to be used to amplify the sound into rehearsals as early as possible, so that the operator can be well prepared for the full range of performance changes. This will also reduce the time needed in the theatre, plotting the sound, although adjustments will inevitably have to be made for the new acoustic.

Plotting

The sound to be made live must be plotted on paper like a normal sound cue, this information coming from rehearsals or a plotting session. As well as a good knowledge of the sound to be amplified live, it is important that the sound operator has a paper plot, with levels, tone adjustments and so on, from which to start.

Plotting music

At a plotting session involving the playing of music the sound designer works with the director, musical director, composer, conductor, or possibly the performers themselves, to achieve the correct setting of microphone levels etc. for each piece of music. This can take a long time, and if possible such a session should be arranged well in advance so that any problems arising can be ironed out, and if necessary further sessions called.

OPERATION

During the performance itself the sound operator should be placed in a suitable position to monitor the sound as the audience hears it. If this is not possible the operator can monitor the sound on headphones as it goes to the amplifier, that is, post-mix. This is, of course, only feasible if *all*

the sound is to be amplified.

The operator makes constant judgements as to the quality of the sound, and adjusts levels and tone controls accordingly. With practice the operator's response seems automatic.

Mixing live sound for the first time is obviously very nerve-racking. The beginner should take things gently, making no large changes.

One of the biggest problems of live sound mixing is feedback.

FEEDBACK

This phenomenon is caused by the amplified sound coming from a loudspeaker being sent into a microphone and back through the sound system. The result is a very high-pitched scream, also called howl round. If left unchecked this process continues for ever, the scream increases until it is uncomfortable to listen to, and can damage equipment.

Feedback does not occur if the microphone points at a speaker that is being used, but not to project amplified sound.

IDENTIFYING AND AVOIDING FEEDBACK

You can spot the early stages of feedback by listening for a slight ringing in the higher frequencies, particulary the sound of the letter 's'.

To avoid it, always position and direct loudspeakers away from microphones. Loudspeakers relaying sound to the audience should be placed in front of the microphones on stage, and facing away from them. Microphones that are perilously near speakers should be directional so that they only pick up sound from where they point and not any coming from the nearby speaker.

If feedback occurs the immediate remedy is to drop the level of the microphone which is causing it. If this cannot be identified use the mixer's master fader to drop all levels, then, using pre-fade, listen to and check each microphone individually.

Using more bass than treble can also allow the microphone to be raised to a higher level before feedback occurs.

CHAPTER 23

SOUND EFFECT SOURCES

The noises required to make up a theatre sound effects tape can be myriad. They may be straightforward or highly complicated mixes. They may be sounds that we are supposed to recognize or entirely new and invented noises. Even everyday sounds can be difficult to record, or it can seem impossible to find existing ones. This section lists all the most likely sources to use to get the sound you want.

To help yourself in future it is a good idea to catalogue the effects used, after each production has finished.

Note: The word effects is often abbreviated to FX.

LIVE SOUND EFFECTS

Some sound effects may sound better, or be easier to cue, if they are performed live. An obvious example is the sound of a telephone – it is quite easy to acquire a phone that really works and usually far more convincing. The same is true of stage guns.

Some offstage noises may also sound better if the noise is actually made live from offstage. This is partly why stage pyrotechnics are used for explosions, especially maroons (firecrackers). (See page 73.) Other examples include the opening and shutting of doors, the noise of a crash of furniture, breaking glass, a gun shot, people shouting, talking, crying etc.

Many of these sounds can also be cheated offstage. It is not necessary to build a whole door to make the sound of a door slamming; a miniature works just as well and is much easier to move and store. The noise of breaking glass is traditionally produced by rattling glass inside an enclosed box, which is both realistic and safe.

Before the invention of recording equipment some very complicated devices were used to produce offstage noise effects. Some of these and many more modern ones are illustrated here.

We can define the live sound effect as coming from any object on stage that makes a sound with no need of modern recording equipment – tape recorders, microphones, etc. There are two kinds of such devices:

■ a stage prop that has to appear to make the correct sound – e.g. a telephone
■ a stage machine that makes the noise of a sound effect – e.g. a wind machine.

SOUND PROPS

These are objects that appear to be the source of the sound: radios, TV sets etc. They can be cheated by the placing of a loudspeaker close to where the source of the sound is supposed to be. But it is more effective if the props themselves actually work. The best example of this is the stage telephone. Of course, the telephone does not carry any real sound, but if it rings and stops ringing when the receiver is lifted, using its own mechanism, then the interaction between the actor and it does not need careful cueing, and the sound effect cannot possibly be anything but authentic. Such devices are made effective in a variety of ways.

Telephones
These run on small voltages which can easily be generated from a transformer. The ringing pulse can either be generated from another transformer or simply by turning the initial source on and off by hand.

Radios
The radio's own loudspeaker may be usable and is easily intercepted from within. It could also be replaced with a more powerful speaker of the same size.

TV sets
These can be treated in much the same way as a radio. Great care must be taken, as a television can store a large electrical charge even when not connected to the mains. Also take care with the tube, which is a vacuum device and if broken or cracked can implode. If in doubt keep well away.

Doorbells/buzzers
These devices are easy to install and cheap to buy. Mains-supplied models are preferable as they do not rely on a battery being checked. They are also easy to make.

SOUND MACHINES

Before the days of recorded and amplified sound stage effects were produced by machines. Some of these can still prove very useful and effective. They may also be less expensive. Many of these machines can also be used as a source for recorded sound effects.

Doors
As described previously this is a miniature door which can be made to creak like a real one, and be fitted with locks, chains, etc. The most famous theatrical door slam is that occurring in the final moments of Ibsen's The Doll's House.

Footsteps
All this needs is a tray of some suitable substance, and a performer who walks or runs on the spot to make the sound effect. Different substances in the tray will sound like gravel, snow, mud etc.

Wind
The wind machine has a piece of canvas held taut over a circular drum. A handle revolves the drum which slides under the canvas to sound like the wind. Simply turning the handle at different speeds produces different wind speeds. This device is featured in Vaughan Williams' Symphony Antarctica.

Wind machine

Rain
This can be simulated very simply by dropping rice or sand on to a tambourine or some similar reverberating surface.

The traditional rain machine consists of a cylinder filled with a few dried peas and with fixed wooden pegs along its length. The cylinder pivots and the peas run to the other end, hitting the pegs. The resulting noise sounds like rain. The greater the angle of the machine the faster the peas fall and the heavier the rain sounds.

Water effects
The rain machine described above can also produce the sound of running water if filled with a greater number of dried peas.

Sea noises can be made by swishing dried peas around a tambourine or small drum.

Small containers of water offstage can also be amplified to sound like much larger water effects: waterfalls, typhoons etc.

Thunder

This was traditionally created with the rolling of a cannon ball down a wooden shute. Obstructions along the shute caused louder rumbles.

Thunder is also produced by shaking a large hung metal sheet. Galvanized-iron produces the correct deep rumble. Smaller sheets produce higher sounds.

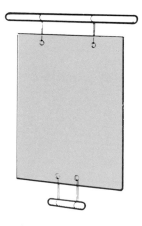

Crashes

Off-stage crashes can be organized by the controlled dropping of various objects. Breaking glass can be dangerous so an enclosed box with broken glass in it can be used offstage for this effect. This is called a crash box. To avoid making of mess crash boxes are often used with other contents such as metal or crockery.

Fire

The noise of fire is difficult to make offstage but with amplification Cellophane being rustled can be used.

RECORDING REAL SOUND EFFECTS

Many sounds, such as background chatter, traffic and rushing water, are easy to record from real life. Others – thunder, rain, sea and general background noises – can be very difficult but not impossible. A few – warfare or earthquake – will, one hopes, remain unobtainable.

Remember that sounds can be recorded to represent something other than what they really are: a running tap can sound like a waterfall. Further examples of creating sounds are given below.

RECORDED SOUND EFFECT SOURCES

The first thing to check when using a commercially produced sound effects record or pre-recorded music is that the copyright is not going to be infringed.

Second, check that any payment due for its use is made. In the UK this means submitting a form for each production to the Performing Rights Society. This society grades the use of sound effects in different ways, and charges amateurs and professionals different rates. Charges can be quite nominal.

The BBC in the UK, and CBS in the USA have a remarkably comprehensive catalogue of sound effects records, cassette tapes and, recently, compact discs. These recordings make up the backbone of many an effects tape. Some examples: all the atmospheric sounds (wind, rain etc), warfare, cars, aircraft, animals, machines, and many different background noises – airports, factories, hospitals. They also do strange and unusual sounds: two of the BBC records are called- *Comedy Sounds* and *Sounds of Death and Horror*. There are thousands of sounds available in each collection.

ELECTRONIC SOUNDS

Some sound effects, as well as music, can be produced on electronic synthesizers and similar keyboards. Some electronic machines – emulators – are specifically made to imitate the sound of others things. Although their primary function may be to emulate other musical instruments they can usually be used in a variety of other ways.

Electronic instruments can be used to produce weird, wonderful and magical sounds, but they can also make other more specific noises such as most machines, telephones, helicopters, cars, guns etc. They can also prove effective for some atmospheric sounds. They can do imitations of some animal sounds: roars and stampedes, bees buzzing, and birds singing.

CREATING SOUND TAPES

Finally, here is a list of examples of how a whole world of sound can be built up in many different ways. In all cases these are only suggestions, and only the beginning of the work. Remember that too much sound can be a distraction and annoyance to the audience. Once a scene has been established with the appropriate sounds let them gently fade away as the action progresses.

Ship breaking apart

The first scene of *The Tempest:*
■ amplified sound of twisting rope and breaking wood
■ plus sound effect of coffins and portcullis opening from sound effects records
■ plus amplified sound of polystyrene being broken apart or slid over a polished surface
■ plus men and women shouting and screaming
■ plus wind, sea, rain, thunder, explosions.

The end of the world

The end of many new plays e.g. *The Hellfire Club* by Andrew Rashleigh:
■ sound effect of a gradually building note (slow down a note from a musical or electronic instrument)
■ plus wind and thunder, possibly distorted and speeded up
■ plus distant screams
■ plus distant sound of riot, warfare or general panic
■ plus noise of earthquake (sound effects records).

Summer sounds

For example *A Midsummer Night's Dream:*
■ intermittent sound of bees buzzing
■ plus light summer birdsong
■ plus occasional distant dog barking
■ plus quiet sound of nearby stream.

City sounds

Background to many modern plays – *The Odd Couple* among others:
■ traffic sounds
■ plus occasional sirens passing
■ plus the occasional dog barking
■ plus the distant sound of shouting
■ plus occasional sound of music.

CHAPTER 24

SOUND DESIGN EXAMPLES

Here are two examples showing how a sound rig may be designed to suit a certain production. One is quite straightforward, the other is not. In each case the amount of equipment used is, of course, debatable. All the ideas used to create each design are taken from the preceding chapters.

THE ODD COUPLE – Neil Simon

This production has a box set and follows the traditional idea that the stage set is a normal room with the 'fourth wall' removed. Such a production generally calls for naturalistic sound effects and the diagram shows how this is could be achieved.

EQUIPMENT

LOUDSPEAKERS x 5
MICROPHONES x 0
PRACTICALS x 1
TAPE DECKS × 2 (background noise to be continuous)
MIXER – 4 in to 5 (with tone and panning controls)

1 Speakers behind set for exterior noises of city: traffic, sirens, rain. Speakers pointed to cross the stage and the auditorium. Sound tape traffic, pans left to right and right to left.

2 Speaker behind set wall down stage right for sounds from radio.

3 Television not thought to be very important so upstage left. General exterior speaker also used for television.

4 Real two-way intercom bought for door. Extended to area out of hearing but near stage for other user. (Alternatively a small speaker could have been mounted in the door with either pre-recorded tape played through it or an actor offstage using a microphone.)

5 Speakers in auditorium for introductory music. Nice feature being to pan the clear stereo pre-show music on to the radio speaker with lights up. Adjust the tone controls while doing so to get a tinnier quality from the radio.

6 Auditorium speakers are positioned over the proscenium so that they have a good shot at the whole depth of the audience, in which case they could also be fed a little of the background noise to catch the audience seated at some distance. A sound delay system should not be necessary because the speakers are in the direction from which sound should be coming anyway.

7 Practical telephone.

MACBETH –
William Shakespeare

This production is set on a thrust stage with the audience on three sides. The majority of the audience is, however, still in front of the stage. Here is how this production was dealt with.

EQUIPMENT

LOUDSPEAKERS x 12
MICROPHONES x 4 rifle, 4 radio, 2 on stands.
PRACTICALS X 0
TAPE DECKS x 2 for overlapping effects.
MIXER – 14 in to 12. See note below.
ECHO MACHINE

Note: A smaller mixer could be used if tape decks play in mono, speakers are paired, and microphones switched for use at different times. At a stretch the mixer could be 4 in to 2 ! This would certainly keep the operator busy, but might lead to inaccuracies and mistakes.
Great care will have to be taken to avoid feedback. The microphone sources on stage may have to be relayed only to the speakers at the rear of the stage and auditorium.

1 Speakers behind the set for upstage sound effects: distant battle, offstage screams etc.

2 Speakers above the thrust for atmospherics: storm, thunder, howling wind. Two speakers directed at main block, two for sides.

3 Speakers to the rear of the main seating block to reinforce atmospheric sounds and place the main seating block as much in the centre of the action as those nearer and around the stage.

4 Speaker hidden underneath set for further atmospherics. The bass boom of a thunder clap vibrates the wooden stage and the auditorium very effectively. (Stage maroons (firecrackers) could also be used here.)

5 Speaker hidden in witches' cauldron for initial voices of apparitions. Speaker connection concealed on stage and to be connected by stage management during scene change.

6 Rifle microphones flown above the stage to pick up certain parts of the play which are to be relayed through an echo machine to create weird sounds in witches' scenes, and gentle echo in certain castle scenes.

7 Witches to wear radio microphones for some of weird sounds.

8 Macbeth has radio microphone to allow for voice enhancement during soliloquies.

9 Microphones offstage to allow actors to voice-over the apparitions (these could be recorded).

CHAPTER 25

PROBLEM-
SOLVING

These sections deal with problems commonly come across in theatre sound – not only with the answers but, more importantly, the short cuts! A point to start: always label faulty equipment, otherwise in the rush to get on with work it can too easily be recycled back into use, and waste still more time.

NO SOUND FROM A TAPE DECK

Check that you have the correct tape and are in the correct place on it. Check that the tape is properly threaded and runs easily under the head guard. Check that the tape is not twisted. Check the connections from the machine and into the mixer.

VERY LOW SOUND LEVEL

Check that the mixer is properly set up, particularly the microphone impedance setting. Check that all the speakers are working properly. Check all connections.

NO SOUND AT ALL

Check that all the equipment is switched on. Check that the source is properly functioning, that is, the tape is properly threaded and not twisted. Check all the connections, in particular the microphone connections. Check fuses on loudspeakers. Check no inhibits are in use on the mixer, that is that the master faders are not down, or the channels incorrectly switched.

ONLY ONE TAPE DECK TO USE IN PERFORMANCE

Use the different tape tracks to provide different sounds to different channels on the mixer.
Use a cassette player to provide music cues, or long low-quality cues like background noises.

MAKING A LONG CUE AVOIDING MANY EDITS

Make a sound loop and record it on to another tape deck. (See page 104.)

ONLY ONE TAPE DECK FOR A LONG TAPE CUE

To prevent many edits use the tape tracks to overlap sound recording and play back the cue in mono.

NOT ENOUGH AMPLIFIERS

Pair speakers where possible. Install a simple switching board as a patch panel so that at different times the amplified signal can be switched to different speakers. (See page 94.)

LOSING AN AMPLIFIER DURING PERFORMANCE

Re-direct sound cues through other amplifiers by allocating new outputs on the mixer. Make the judgement with the DSM as to whether it is better to hear the sound from the wrong speaker or not at all! If possible re-patch speakers to remaining amplifiers, thereby pairing speakers, taking care not to overload the amplifier. (See page 96.)

MIXER HAS INSUFFICIENT OUTPUTS

Use sound patching system.
Pair speakers where possible.

NOT ABLE TO AFFORD RADIO MICROPHONES

Try allocating directional microphones to pick up the performers, possibly concealing them in the set.
Suggest to the director that the style of the piece would not be greatly changed by the use of hand-held microphones but that the sound quality would.
Mike the whole stage, possibly using float microphones across the stage front.

PERFORMERS NOT USING MICROPHONES PROPERLY

Most performers will wish to use the equipment to its own and their best advantage. Novices will be thankful for tactful instruction. Unfortunately many performers believe they know how to handle a microphone after watching pop singers doing so. Unfortunately such people are often miming and also damaging the equipment. Be tactful and demonstrate how in this particular case and with this particular microphone the best sound can be produced. If there are any further problems get the stage manager or director to help.

PROBLEMS WITH INTERFERENCE

See page 99.

PROBLEMS WITH FEEDBACK

See page 110.

SOUND CUE SHEET

——— CHANNEL ———

CUE NO:	TAPE DECK	LEADER	SPEAKER SELECT	LEVEL	E.Q. (TONE)	MASTERS	ACTION/ SUBJECT	NOTES
1	A	Red	1 + 3	6	+ 10 bass	Full	Intro Music	—
2	B	Green	2 + 4	7	− 20 treble	Full	Rain	20 sec. fade in
3	A	Blue	1 thro. to 4	5	+10 mid. +10 treble	8/10	Voice over	10 sec. fade out
4	CARTRIDGE NO. 1.	—	1 + 3	5	—	8/10	Sea	Loop
5	"	"	"	0	"	0	"	20 sec. fade out
5A	B	yellow	1 + 4	5	+ 10 mid. + 10 treble	Full	voice over	10 sec. fade in
6	A	red	1 + 3	7	+ 20 bass	9/10	interval music	NB. only 20 mins.

SOUND CUE SHEET

CHANNEL _____

CUE NO:	TAPE DECK	LEADER	SPEAKER SELECT	LEVEL	E.Q. (TONE)	MASTERS	ACTION/ SUBJECT	NOTES

SHEET NUMBER _____

PRODUCTION _____

OPERATOR _____

CUE	MEM	BOARD ACTION	VISUAL	TIME

CUE NO: _____

PRESET: _____

1	2	3	4	5	6	7	8	9	10	11	12	13	14	15	16	17	18	19	20	21	22	23	24	25	26	27	28	29	30	31	32	33	34	35	36

ACTION: _____   TIME: _____   AFTER CUE: _____

CUE NO: _____

PRESET: _____

1	2	3	4	5	6	7	8	9	10	11	12	13	14	15	16	17	18	19	20	21	22	23	24	25	26	27	28	29	30	31	32	33	34	35	36

ACTION: _____   TIME: _____   AFTER CUE: _____

CUE NO: _____

PRESET: _____

1	2	3	4	5	6	7	8	9	10	11	12	13	14	15	16	17	18	19	20	21	22	23	24	25	26	27	28	29	30	31	32	33	34	35	36

ACTION: _____   TIME: _____   AFTER CUE: _____

The large satin cape undulating in light and smoke created the appearance of flight as Aslan carries the children on his back in The Lion the Witch and the Wardrobe.

The central character is highlighted using steep top light to create skull like features on his face.

Glossary

A

Anti-pros (US) see Front-of-House lights

Apron extension of stage beyond the proscenium

ASM assistant stage manager

Auditorium area in which the audience is accommodated during the performance

B

Backcloth cloth usually painted, suspended from Flies at the rear of the stage

Backing (1) cloth or solid pieces placed behind doorways and other openings on sets to conceal stage machinery and building (2) financial support for a production

Bar horizontally flown rod (usually metal) from which scenery, lighting and other equipment are suspended

Bar bells bells sounded in all front-of-house areas to warn audience that the performance is about to continue. Operated from prompt corner, and so usually written into prompt copy

Barndoor adjustable shutters attached to stage lights to control the area of light covered by a particular lamp

Batten (1) see Bar (2) piece of wood attached to flown cloth to straighten it and keep it taut (3) piece of wood joining two flats (4) a group of stage lights suspended over the stage

Beam light a light with no lens, giving a parallel beam

Beginners call given by deputy stage manager to bring those actors who appear first in the play to the stage

Bifocal spot spotlight with additional shutters to allow hard and soft edges

Black light ultra violet light

Blocking the process of arranging moves to be made by the actor

Board lighting control panel

Book (1) alternative term for the scripts (2) the prompt copy (3) the part of a musical show conducted in dialogue

Book flat two flats hinged together on the vertical

Booking closing a book flat

Boom a vertical lighting bar

Boom arch used to hang a lantern from a boom

Border flown scenic piece designed to conceal the upper part of the stage and its machinery or equipment

Box set setting which encloses the acting area on three sides. Conventionally in imitation of a room in which the fourth wall has been removed

Brace portable support for flats

Bridge walkway above the stage used to reach stage equipment

C

Call (1) warning given at intervals to technicians and actors that they are needed on stage (2) notice of the time at which actors will be required to rehearse a particular scene

Callboard notice board on which calls and all other information relevant to the production should be posted

Cans headsets used for communication and co-ordination of technical departments during a performance

Centreline imaginary line drawn from rear to front of stage and dividing it exactly in half. Marked as CL on stage plans

Channel a circuit in the lighting or sound system

Chase a repeated sequence of changing lighting states

Check to diminish the intensity of light or sound on stage

Cinemoid a colour medium or filter

Circuit the means by which a lantern is connected to a dimmer or patch panel

Clamp C or G clamps are attached to lights to fasten them to bars

Cleat fixing on the back of flats to allow them to be laced together (cleated) with a sash line or cleat line. Also a metal fly rail to which ropes are tied

Clothscene scene played before downstage drop or tabs, while a major scene change takes place

Colour call the list of coloured gels required for a lighting design taken from the plan of the lighting design

Colour frame holder for the colour medium or filter in front of the light

Colour Medium translucent filter material placed in front of lights to give a coloured illumination

Colour wheel in lighting, a device attached to lamps which, when rotated, charges the colour medium through which the light is shown

Come down (1) instruction to actor to move towards the audience (2) instruction to lower intensity of sound or light (3) end of performance; time when curtain comes down

Corner plate triangle of plywood used to reinforce the corners of a flat

Counterweights mechanical system used for raising and lowering flown scenery

Counterweight flying the system of flying scenery, lights etc., whereby the flown item is balanced by counterweights

Crossfade the practice of moving to a new lighting or sound effect without intervening darkness or silence; one effect fades out simultaneously with the new one's being brought into play

Crossover (1) the device on a sound system that routes the sound of the correct pitch to the correct part of the loudspeaker; (2) the space behind the stage setting or below the stage through which actors can get from one side of the stage to the other without being seen by the audience

Cue (1) verbal or physical signal for an actor to enter or speak a line (2) point at which an effect is executed or business takes place

Cue light box with two lights, red and green, which warn an actor or technician to standby (red) and then do (green) whatever is required of them. Ensures greater precision when visibility or audibility is limited

Cue sheet list of particular effects executed by one department in a production

Cue-to-cue rehearsal of technical effects in a production with actors. The scene is rehearsed in sections beginning with a cue for standby, and concluding when the effect is finished

Curtain call process of actors appearing at the end of the play to receive audience applause. Formerly actors were called before the curtain by the audience

Curtain speech out of character address to the audience by a cast member or participant

Curtain up (1) time at which a play begins (2) a call given to the company to warn them the performance has begun

Cut cloth vertical scenic piece cut to reveal more scenery behind it. Most common in musicals

Cutting list list of materials required for scenery and set construction together with the correct dimensions of the pieces

Cyclorama undecorated backing to a stage, usually semi-circular and creating a sense of space and height. Often some theatres have permanent or standing cycloramas which have actually been built. The term is always abbreviated to cyc

D

Dead (1) the point at which a piece of scenery reaches the desired position onstage (2) a redundant production or scenic element

Decibel dB the measurement of volume of sound

Diffusion (colour) used like a gel but to soften and spread the beam of light rather than to colour it. Also called a frost

Dim the process of decreasing the intensity of light onstage

Dimmers the apparatus whereby lights are electrically dimmed

Dip small covered hole in stage floor with electric sockets

Dock area at side or rear of stage where scenery is stored when not in use

Downstage part of stage nearest to audience

Dress circle also known as the circle. Area of seating above the stalls and below the balcony

Dressing items used to decorate a setting

Dress parade the final check of costumes before the first dress rehearsal. The cast parade each of their costumes in order before the Director and Costume Designer so that any final alterations can be made

Drop suspended cloth flown into stage area

DSM deputy stage manager

Dutchman (US) thin piece of material used to cover the cracks between two flats

E

Elevation a working drawing usually drawn accurately and to scale, showing the side view of the set or lighting arrangement

Ellipsoidal the type of reflector used in many profile spots

Entrance (1) place on a set

through which the actor may appear (2) point in the script at which an actor appears

Exit (1) the process of leaving the stage (2) point in the script at which an actor leaves the stage

F

Fader a means of controlling the output level of a lantern (lamp) or amplifier

False proscenium construction placed behind the real theatre proscenium for decorative or practical purposes

Fit-up installation of lighting, technical equipment and scenery onstage when coming into a theatre

Flash-out system to check whether the lights are functioning properly by putting them on one at a time

Flat scenic unit comprised of wood or stretched cloth applied to a timber frame and supported so that it stands vertical to the stage door. Door flats and window flats have these openings in them. Masking flats are placed at the outer edges of the acting area to disguise areas of the stage from the public

Flies area above the stage in which scenery, lighting and other equipment are kept. If whole backdrops are to be stored then the flies should be at least twice the height of the stage opening

Floodlights also called floods. Lights which give a general fixed spread of light

Floorcloth painted canvas sheets placed on the stage floor to give a specific effect

Floor pocket (US) see dip

Flown (1) scenery or equipment which has been suspended above the stage (2) flown pieces are any scenic elements which will be made to appear or disappear from view in sight of the audience

Fly the process of bringing scenery in and out of the stage area vertically

Flying (1) the process of stocking the flies (2) special effects whereby actors are suspended by wires to create the illusion of flying

Fly floor gallery at either side of the stage from which the flies are operated

Floats see footlights

Focusing the process of fixing the exact area to be lit by each light onstage

FOH Front-of-house. Any part of the theatre in front of the proscenium arch

Follow spot light directed at actor which can follow all movements

Footlights lights set into the stage at floor level which throw strong general light into performers' faces downstage

Fourth wall imaginary wall between audience and actors which completes the naturalistic room

French brace support for scenery fixed to stage

Fresnel type of spotlight with a fresnel lens which gives an even field of light with soft edges

Frontcloth see cloth

Front-of-House lights lights hung in front of the proscenium arch

Frost see diffusion

G

Gauze painted cloth screen, opaque when lit from the front, that becomes transparent when lit from behind. Often used at front of stage to diffuse total stage picture

Gel Colour medium introduced before light to alter colour of beam

Get-in/out (US) see fit-up process of bringing scenery into or taking it out of the theatre

Ghost a beam of light which inadvertently leaks from a light and falls where it is not wanted

Gobo (1) screen introduced before a stage light to give a particular image onstage (2) cut out shape that is projected

Green room general area in which cast and crew wait during performance

Grid metal frame from which all flying equipment is suspended

Groundrow raised section of scenery usually depicting bushes rocks etc.

Grouping (US) see blocking

H

Half half hour call. Warning to company given thirty-five minutes before performance

Handprop any prop handled by an actor, such as a handbag, walking stick, umbrella

Hanging attaching flying pieces to appropriate bars

Hook clamp the device that holds a lantern onto a bar

Hot lining the method by which lanterns, bulbs and cables are checked during rigging

House (1) audience (2) in opera, the entire theatre, and by implication, the company

I

Impedance a term for the electrical resistance found in a/c circuits, thus affecting the ability of a cable to transmit sound as electrical pulses. Measured in ohms

In one (US) see clothscene

Inset a small scene set inside a larger one

Iris a device within a lantern which allows a circular beam to be altered through a range of sizes

Iron a fire proof curtain that can be dropped downstage of the tabs in case of fire. Today it is usually made of solid metal and is electrically operated

K

Kill instruction to cease use of particular effect in lighting or sound

L

Ladder a ladder-shapped frame used for hanging side lights. It cannot usually be climbed

Lamp unit of lighting equipment

Lantern see lamp

Left stage left. That part of the stage to the actor's left when he is facing toward the audience

Leg cloth suspended vertically from flies and used to mask sides of stage and small areas within it

Levels (1) indicates intensity or volume of light or sound (2) raised areas onstage used for acting

Limes jargon for follow spots and their operators

Line drawings (US) see technical drawing

Linnebach projector used for projecting a picture from a gel or glass slide onto the set. Often used to give a shadow effect

Load in/out (US) see get in/out

Lose to turn off lighting or sound, or to remove an article from the set

Luminaire international term for lighting equipment. Not restricted to theatrical lighting

M

Marking (1) in use of props or scenery, the deployment of substitutes for the real object during rehearsal (2) in singing, a

means of using the voice with reduced volume and without vocalising extremes of register (3) any account of a role in which the full powers are not being used by the performer in order to save resources

Maroon a pyrotechnic giving the effect of a loud explosion

Mark out the system of lines and objects set on a rehearsal room floor to indicate the exact position of scenery and furniture. Marking out is the process of doing this

Mask to hide or conceal unwanted areas or machinery. Also used to describe one actor obscuring another unintentionally

MD musical director

Memory memory board. An advanced type of lighting control system where the required levels are stored electronically

Mezzanine area of seating above the orchestra and below the balcony. When a theatre has only a single balcony, first several rows are frequently designated the mezzanine

Mixer sound controls desk, used to mix and adjust levels of sounds from various sources

O

Offstage any backstage area not seen by the audience. Most specifically used to indicate the areas at the actor's right and left

OP opposite prompt. Stage Right (US Stage left)

Orchestra (US) see stalls

Out flying term for up

Overture (1) the music which begins a performance (2) a call to the actors and technicians that the performance is about to begin in a musical work

P

PA system the public address or any sound amplification system

Pack a number of flats all stored together

Pan (1) movement of lighting from side to side (2) used to describe water-based stage make-up (pancakes) (3) term (now nearly obsolete) to describe theatre sound installation

Parcan type of lantern which holds a par lamp

Patch border panel a panel at which the circuits governed by individual lighting dimmers can be changed

Perch lighting position concealed behind the proscenium

Periactus a tall, prism-shaped piece of painted scenery which can be revolved to show various phases

Pipe (US) see bar

Places please (US) see beginners

Platform (US) see rostrum

Plot (1) commonly used to describe the action of a play (2) any list of cues for effects used in the play

PM production manager

Practical any object which must do onstage the same job that it would do in life, or any working apparatus e.g. a light switch or water tap (faucet)

Preset (1) used to describe any article placed in its working area before the performance commences (2) also describes a basic lighting state that the audience sees before the action begins

Projector (US) see floodlight

Prompt copy fully annotated copy of the play with all the production details from which the show is run each time it is performed

Properties props. Any item or article used by the actors in performance other than costume and scenery

Props skip basket or cupboard in which props are kept when not in use

Props table table in convenient offstage area on which all properties are left prior to performance and to which they should be returned when dead

Pros proscenium arch the arch which stands between stage and auditorium. A pros arch theatre is a conventional theatre with a proscenium arch, usually without a forestage

PS prompt side. Conventionally meaning stage left, the term now refers only to the side of the stage in which the prompt corner will be found. In the US the PS is generally stage right

Prompt corner desk and console at the side of the stage from which the stage manager runs the show

Pyrotechnics any chemical effects used onstage or in wings to create lighting or special effects

Q

Quarter back stage pre-show call given twenty minutes before curtain up (ie. fifteen minutes before beginners)

R

Rail bottom or top batten of the frame of a flat

Rake the incline of a stage floor away from the horizontal; a raked stage is higher at the upstage end than at the downstage

Readthrough early rehearsal at which the play is read without action. Usually accompanied by discussion

Reflectors the shiny surfaces in the back of lighting equipment which help intensify the beam

Rigging the means of fixing lamps to appropriate bars before lighting a production

Right stage right. That part of the stage to the actor's right when he is facing the audience

Risers the vertical part of a stage step

Rostrum a raised platform sometimes with a collapsible frame used for giving local prominence to certain areas onstage

Run (1) the number of scheduled performances of a work (2) abbreviated form of run through

Runners a pair of curtains parting at the centre and moving horizontally

S

Saturation rig an arrangement of lights in which the maximum number of spotlights is placed in every possible position

Scatter the light outside the main beam of a spot

Scrim (US) see gauze

Seque musical term indicating that one number should go immediately into the next

Set to prepare the stage for action. To set up is to get ready. To set back is to return to the beginning of a given sequence

Shutter device in front of lamp to alter shape of beam

Single purchase counterweight flying system where the cradle travels the same distance as the fly bar's travel. The counterweight frame therefore occupies the full height of the side wall of the stage

Sightlines the angles of visibility from the auditorium

SM stage manager

Snap line chalk line, chalked piece of string which when stretched tight is used for making straight lines on stage

Special piece of lighting equipment whose main function is to perform a particular effect

Spiking see marking

Spill unwanted light onstage

Spot spotlight. Light giving a small circle of light, the dimensions of which can be precisely controlled by focusing

Stagger-run runthrough at which the production is pieced together, aiming at fluency but allowing for corrective stops

Stalls floor level area of seating in the auditorium

Strike instruction to remove any redundant or unnecessary object from stage

Super non-speaking actor not specifically named in the text

Swag curtains or tabs gathered together so they do not hang straight

Switchboard board from which lights are controlled

T

Tabs theatre curtains, most usually the House curtain

Tabtrack metal track on which the tabs run allowing them to open and close

Tallescope extendable ladder on wheels used in rigging and focusing lights and for minor corrections to flown pieces

Teaser short flown border used to mask scenery or equipment

Tech technical rehearsal at which all technical effects are rehearsed in the context of the whole production

Theatre in the Round acting area with audience on all sides

Throw in lighting, the distance between a light source and the object lit

Thrust stage type of stage which projects into the auditorium so that the audience can sit on at least three sides

Tilt the vertical movement of light

Tormentor (US) see teaser

Trap hole cut in stage and concealed by floor allowing access from below. Grave traps are usually double traps creating the illusion of a grave or pit. Once a common part of all theatres traps are now becoming increasingly rare

Trapeze single short hung lighting bar

Treads the flat part of stage steps

Truck movable cradle upon which scenery is placed to facilitate its movement

U

Upstage in a proscenium or thrust stage the area furthest away from the audience

W

Wagon (US) see truck

Walk-through rehearsals at which actors go through entrances, moves and exits to make clear any changes or alterations made necessary through change of cast or venue

Warning bells (US) see Bar bells

Ways the maximum number of combinations of channels on a lighting installation

Wings the sides of the stage concealed from the audience's view

Work-out in a dance or movement rehearsal, a vigorous session to prepare the body for specific work

Workshop any non-performing backstage area of a theatre

Workshop performance a performance in which maximum effort goes towards acting and interpretation rather than sets or costumes

Musical theatre special glossary

Andante walking space

Allegro happily, lightly

Allargando getting broader

Coda last section of music, often in a different tempo or mood

Cadence the resolving chords in music

Largo broadly

Lento slowly

Maestoso majestically

Presto fast

Aria solo, usually reflective in content

Duet musical number for two singers

Trio three singers

Quartet four singers

Ensemble (1) together (2) place in which all the characters all sing together

Finale (1) the end (2) by extension, a musical sequence which ends each act, often comprising different musical material but having an overall shape

MD musical director

Band parts the individual copies required by each player in an orchestra and containing only the notes for their particular instrument.

BIBLIOGRAPHY

Listed below are a representative selection of books for each of the titles in this series.

In the United Kingdom Spotlight publish annually *Contacts*, a complete guide to the British Stage, TV, Screen and Radio (7 Leicester Place, London WC2. Tel: 071 437 7631)

In the United States the Theatre Communications Group Inc. (TCG) (355 Lexington Avenue, New York, NY 10017. Tel: 212 697 5230) has a publications department which publishes not only plays and books but also a monthly magazine of news and features called *American Theatre*. It also publishes an employment bulletin for the performing arts called Art SEARCH.

Bentley, Eric *Theory of the Modern Stage*, London, 1968

Brook, Peter *The Empty Space*, London, 1985

Brown, John R *Drama and the Theatre*, London, 1971

Hoggett, Chris *Stage and the Theatre*, London, 1971

Oren Parker, Smith, W L, Harvey R *Scene Design and Stage Lighting*, London, 1979

Stanlislawski, K *An Actor Prepares*, London, 1981

Costume and Make-up

Barton, Lucy *Historic Costume for the Stage*, Boston, 1938

Barton, Lucy *Period Patterns*, Boston, 1942

Corson, Richard *Fashions in Hair*, London, 1985

Corson, Richard *Stage Make-up*, New York 1960

Cunnington, Phillis and Lucas, Catherine *Occupational Costume in England*, London, 1967

Directing a Play

Berry, Cicely *Voice and the Actor*, London and New York, 1974

Hagen, Uta and Frankel, Haskel *Respect for Acting*, New York, 1980

Hodgson, John and Richards, Ernest *Improvisation*, London, 1978; New York, 1979

Nicoll, A *The Development of the Theatre*, London and New York, 1966

Willett, John *The Theatre of Bertolt Brecht*, London, 1983; New York, 1968

Lighting and Sound

Bentham, Fredrick *Art of Stage Lighting*, London, 1980; New York, 1968

Burris-Meyer, H and Mallory, V *Sound in the Theatre*, New York, 1979

Moore, J E *Design for Good Acoustics*, London, 1961; New York, 1979

Pilbrow, Richard *Stage Lighting*, London and New York, 1979

Reid, Francis *Stage Lighting Handbook*, London, 1982; New York, 1976

Stage Design and Properties

Govier, Jacquie *Create Your Own Stage Props*, London and New York, 1984

Leacroft, Richard and Helen *Theatre & Playhouse*, London, 1984

Molinari, Cesare *Theatre Through the Ages*, London and New York, 1975

Oren Parker, W L Smith, Harvey, R *Scene Design and Stage Lighting* London and New York, 1979

Stage Management and Theatre Administration

Baker, Hendrik *Stage Management and Theatre Craft, (3rd Edition)*, London and New York, 1981

Bond, David *Stage Management: A Gentle Art*, London 1991

Crampton, Esme *A Handbook of the Theatre*, London and New York, 1980

Gruver, Bert *The Stage Manager's Handbook*, New York, 1972

Reid, Francis *The Staging Handbook*, New York, 1978

SUPPLIERS AND STOCKISTS

Listed below are a representative selection of suppliers and stockists.

UNITED KINGDOM

Costume, Props and Make-Up

Angels and Bermans
40 Camden Street
London NW1 0DX
Tel: 0171 387 0999
Fax: 0171 383 5603

Bapty and Co. Ltd (weapon hire)
703 Harrow Road
London NW10 5NY
Tel: 0181 969 6671
Fax: 0181 960 1106

Borovick Fabrics Ltd (theatrical)
16 Berwick Street
London W1V 3RG
Tel: 0171 437 2180/0520
Fax: 0171 494 4646

Bristol Old Vic Hire
Units 1 and 2
Hayward Road Industrial Estate
Staple Hill
Bristol BS16 4NT
Tel: 0117 970 1026

Brodie and Middleton (dyes, canvas, metal powders and other paints)
68 Drury Lane
London WC2B 5SP
Tel: 0171 836 3289
Fax: 0171 497 8425

Freed of London Ltd (theatrical shoes)
94 St Martin's Lane
London WC2N 4AS
Tel: 0171 240 0432
Fax: 0171 240 3061

Laurence Corner (period hats and other unusual clothing)
62 Hampstead Road
London NW1 2NU
Tel: 0171 813 1010
Fax: 0171 813 1413

Lighting and Sound

DHA Lighting Ltd
3 Jonathan Street
London SE11 5NH
Tel: 0171 582 3600
Fax: 0171 582 4779

Jim Laws Lighting
West End Lodge
Wrentham
Beccles
Suffolk NR34 7NH
Tel: 0502 675 264
Fax: 0502 675 565

MAC (Sound Hire)
1 and 2 Attenburys Park Road
Altrincham
Cheshire WA14 5QE
Tel: 0161 969 8311
Fax: 0161 962 9423

Northern Stage Services Ltd
Unit 1, Trent Industrial Estate
Duchess Street
Shaw
Oldham OL2 7UT
Tel: 0170 684 9469
Fax: 0170 684 0138

Strand Lighting
Grant Way
Isleworth
Middlesex TW7 5QD
Tel: 0181 560 3171
Fax: 0181 568 2103

Theatre Project Sound Services
13 Field Way
Bristol Road
Greenford
Middlesex UB6 8UN
Tel: 0181 813 1112
Fax: 0181 566 6365

White Light Electrics Ltd
57 Filmer Road
London SW6 7JF
Tel: 0171 731 3291
Fax: 0171 371 0806

Stage Equipment

British Harlequin
Kent House
High Street
Farningham DA4 0DT
Tel: 0132 286 5288
Fax: 0132 286 4803

CCT lighting
Hindle House
Traffic Street
Nottingham NG2 1NE
Tel: 0115 986 2722
Fax: 0115 986 2546

Flint Hire and Supply Ltd
35 Queen's Row
London SE17 2PX
Tel: 0171 703 9786
Fax: 0171 708 4189

Northern Light
39 Assembly Street
Leith
Edinburgh EH6 7RG
Tel: 0131 553 2383
Fax: 0131 553 3296

Northern Light
79 Loanbank Quadrant
Govan
Glasgow G51 3HZ
Tel: 0141 440 1771
Fax: 0141 445 4406

Rex Howard (Drapes) Ltd
Acton Park Industrial Estate
Eastman Road
The Vale
London W3 7QS
Tel: 0181 740 5881
Fax: 0181 740 5994

UNITED STATES

It is impossible to give a comprehensive list of suppliers and stockists in the space available. Those wishing to find a specific supplier should consult *Theatre Crafts Directory* (P.O. Box 470, Mt Morris, Illinois 61054 - 0470). This publication gives a comprehensive list of suppliers for costume fabric, electrical supplies, dance-wear, curtains and drapes, film equipment, and flameproofing. It even lists about 50 suppliers of feathers for theatrical costumes!

Costume, Props and Make-Up

Norcosto Inc.
3203 North Highway 100
Minneapolis
Minnesota 55422
Tel: 612 533 2791
Fax: 612 533 3718

Stagecraft Industries
5051 North Lagoon Avenue
Portland
Oregon 97217
Tel: 503 286 1600
Fax: 503 286 3345

Tobins Lake Studios
7030 Old US 23
Brighton
Michigan 48116
Tel: 810 229 6666
Fax: 810 229 0221

Wolf and Co.
4301 Bryan Street 309
Dallas
Texas 75204
Tel: 214 823 1880
Fax: 214 823 5659

Lighting and Sound

Electronics Diversified
1675 NW 216th Avenue
Hillsboro
Oregon 97124
Tel: 503 645 5533
Fax: 503 629 9877

Hub Electric Inc.
6207 Commercial Road
Crystal Lake
Illinois 60014
Tel: 708 530 6860
Fax: 815 455 1499

Showco Inc.
201 Regal Row
Dallas
Texas 75247
Tel: 214 819 3100/630 1188
Fax: 214 630 5867

Stage Equipment

Peter Albrecht Corporation
6250 Industrial Court
Greendale
Wisconsin 53129 - 2432
Tel: 414 421 6630
Fax: 414 421 9091